NEWSPAPERING IN THE OLD WEST

"Our duty is to keep the universe thoroughly posted concerning murders and street fights, and balls, and theaters, and pack-trains, and churches, and lectures, and school-houses, and city military affairs, and highway robberies, and Bible societies, and haywagons, and a thousand other things which it is in the province of local reporters to keep track of and magnify into undue importance for the instruction of the readers of this great daily newspaper."

Mark Twain
Territorial Enterprise
Virginia City, Nevada Territory

Division of Manuscripts, Library, University of Oklahoma

Newspapering in the OLD WEST

A Pictorial History of Journalism and Printing on the Frontier.

by Robert F. Karolevitz.

BONANZA BOOKS · NEW YORK

This edition published by Bonanza Books,
a division of Crown Publishers, Inc.,
by arrangement with Superior Publishing Company
A   B   C   D   E   F   G   H

LIBRARY OF CONGRESS CARD CATALOGUE NUMBER 65-23450

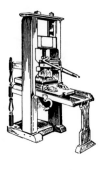

(Title page) The shop of the *Maysville* (Okla.) *News* characterized the marginal operation of many early-day newspapers. Hand-crank presses, pot-bellied stoves and the printer's bed in the adjoining room were typical of the equipment of hundreds of frontier journals. (Opposite title page) The Statue of Liberty adorned the office of Tucson's *Arizona Citizen*, shown in this photo from the Arizona Pioneers' Historical Society.

Union Pacific Railroad

Dedication.

THE MEN AND WOMEN WHO MADE THIS BOOK POSSIBLE are no longer among us. They came upon the scene, made their marks on history—feebly or indelibly—and then passed on.

Few are known by name today. A mere handful became famous; fewer yet became wealthy—and, if so, seldom as journalists. For some it was the "easy way out," less demanding physically than panning for gold or hewing timbers. For others it was a high calling.

To those editors, publishers, printers and devils who brought the news to the frontier, then, this volume is dedicated, not so much in honor of what they wrote or how many ems they set, but in recognition of the courage and doggedness with which they established the Fourth Estate in the Old West!

A Foreword.

Close on the trail of the prospector's burro, the settlers' oxen and the smoke-belching engines of the first transcontinental trains, came the chroniclers of the Old West.

These were the editors, the publishers and printers of the frontier newspapers, the irrepressible—often rag-tag—criers of good news and bad.

Wherever men wandered beyond the Mississippi, they craved—even demanded—the news from "back East," the latest intelligence about the wilderness ahead and the current happenings of the immediate settlements to which gold, timber, verdant soil or army orders had brought them.

In the beginning these newspapers were much the same, limited by equipment, supplies and the abilities of their producers. But as the West developed, the frontier gazettes which survived the great odds stacked against them took on individual personalities and appearances to fill their niches in history.

This book is not meant to be an academic dates-and-places report of the pioneer journals of Western America. While great pains have been taken to establish historical authenticity, the author's chief goal has been to recreate the flavor and the atmosphere of newspapering on the frontier.

Newspaper offices on the frontier were the centers of interest, the sources of information and entertainment. Here the men gathered to exchange tidbits, to argue politics, to regale the editor. This scene at the office of *The Kingman* (Kans.) *Mercury* in 1880 was repeated hundreds of times in towns, camps and villages from the Mississippi to the Pacific Ocean during the long, monotonous decades when diversion was limited, drudgery commonplace and the future lay always just beyond the horizon.

The word "frontier" has been interpreted loosely. This story covers not only the first bold plunges into "Indian country" and the vast unsettled expanse west of the Mississippi, but it includes, too, the development which occurred once the wilderness had been conquered. That way this report is able to cover the growth of newspapers from the hand-set, hand-fed chronicles of a romantic era to still a new frontier: the age of mechanization.

The research involved here has uncovered many sweeping generalities about six-gun editors as rugged, talented, incorrupt defenders of freedom and truth—but the fact of the matter is that the men who first brought newspapers to readers on

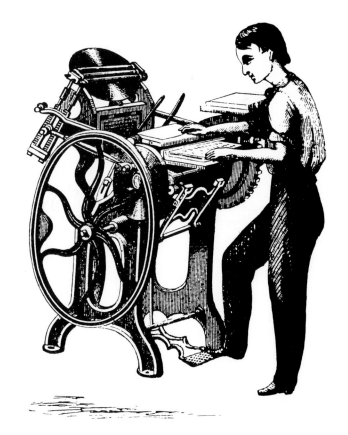

tree stumps and placer chutes ran the spectrum from good to bad, from brilliant to dull, from success to total failure.

Like the sutler, the farrier and candlestick maker, they followed the magnetic trail toward the setting sun, stopping—as if by instinct—at the camp or village to which fate had led them. There they unloaded their crude hand-presses, "laid their cases" and set about their task of informing and entertaining an anxious news-starved populace.

On many occasions the editor and printer were one and the same individual. Generally he faced conditions almost as difficult as those confronting the frontier doctor and dentist. That his ultimate product was as good as it was is another of those miracles of history.

Today the yellowed volumes and sometimes tattered single surviving copies of frontier newspapers provide our most valued link with one of this nation's most romantic periods of vision and achievement. This book seeks to underscore these contributions made to the American heritage by the men and women who hand-spiked the leaden characters, who inked the iron-bound forms and who ultimately delivered the news to subscribers in sod houses, log cabins, lusty saloons and aromatic livery stables.

By comparison, their returns were meager and their labors long, but in the end they left their mark on the annals of the frontier—for what they imprinted upon paper is truly the history of the Old West!

ROBERT F. KAROLEVITZ

Visalia Times-Delta

Cluttered and dimly-lit, the backshops of most early-day newspapers were much the same. Yet, the men who worked at the stones, the cases and the clanking presses were proud of their talent and their product. Printers of the *Visalia* (Calif.) *Daily Times* posed for this turn-of-the-century photo with Sunday shirts and neckties.

Acknowledgments.

ONE OF THE MOST DIFFICULT sections to write in a book of this type is an expression of appreciation for succor, sympathy and services rendered. Not that it is so difficult to say "thank you," but in time so many people become involved that it is difficult to include them all without issuing a second volume.

Wherever I went in search of pictures and material, I received excellent cooperation from librarians, historical society researchists, schools of journalism, newspapermen, printers, interested friends and a few complete strangers.

To them all I owe a debt of gratitude!

Needless to say, there are a special few who deserve individual mention:

William O. Thorniley, whose collection of antique type faces helped give this volume its vintage appearance; Al Salisbury, a publisher with patience; Emmet F. Billings, who provided artistic cartography; Ed Groshell, a newspaperman and friend who started the whole thing; Scott Wallace, who aided and abetted.

Thomas H. Heuterman, for special assistance on the *Frontier Index* story; James W. Phillips, for myriad reasons; Windsor A. Straw, for enthusiastic encouragement when it was needed most, and lastly, my wife, Phyllis, who nagged tactfully and who really is responsible that the manuscript finally got out of the typewriter.

Washington Newspaper Publishers Association

The men who printed the first issue of the *Montesano* (Wash.) *Vidette* on February 1, 1883, re-enacted the scene almost a half-century later. J. E. Calder, with the flowing beard, was a co-founder. His printer's devil (shown here with the two-handed ink brayer) was W. H. Bush. They used an Army press, a small portable model with which the military issued orders and bulletins in the field during the mid-1800s.

Quills, Type Sticks and Six-Guns.

"Ministers are not more addicted to dissipation than the men of other professions. A few of the Kalloch type take gin toddies and liberties with females, but the great majority of them are as good as lawyers and doctors. If you want a true Christian, marry an editor."

The Dakota Democrat
Sioux Falls City, D.T., 1859

J UST WHO WAS THE FRONTIER EDITOR? Romantically, he has been visualized as a bewhiskered champion of liberty, torch-carrier for justice, seeker of truth and author of the homespun phrase.

Somehow the writers of fiction have managed to conjure for him an image of great wisdom,

morality beyond reproach and bravery without peer. In actuality, he was none of these things

—and all of them. It would be difficult to fabricate a composite editor of Old West journalism. At best the creation would only be a broadbrush replica because the men who wielded the quill pens, set the countless ems of body type and activated the toggle joints on the Washington hand-presses were of all ages, all types and all shades of moral fibre.

(Opposite page) Courtesy Oregon State Press Association

(Sketch by Bob Wandesforde)

Seattle First-National Bank (Gus Asplund)

Too often history books and family albums give us a distorted view of the men who actually braved the frontier. Those who made it to a ripe old age, grew beards and then had their pictures taken. But mostly frontier journalism was a young man's game. It took physical stamina, a minimum of family responsibilities and, in many instances, a little foolhardiness. At first, the opportunities for financial gain were limited, and editorial columns were filled with plaintive pleas such as this one in *The Dakota Republican:* "Good wood—four foot or stove length—received as welcomely as cash." In time, however, as communities stabilized, some editors and publishers achieved a certain amount of pecuniary success.

The path to fame and fortune was jammed with obstacles, however. The lure of Eldorado caused many would-be editors to drop their type-sticks

Above is an artist's concept of the shop of the *Seattle Gazette,* the Puget Sound city's first newspaper. Few frontier editors worked in such comfort. Hardly any of them wore cuff links at the cases, and those who had more than dirt underfoot were fortunate.

The Kansas State Historical Society

For decades, frontier newspapers were hand-set, one letter at a time, by tireless printers who stood at their type cases for hours on end. Once the paper was printed, each individual letter had to be "distributed" so that the process could begin all over again. This derby-clad typographer toiled for the *Russell* (Kans.) *Record.*

and grab up gold pans. The bottle took its toll. Mostly, though, the tediousness of the job separated the indolent, the get-rich-quick schemers and the physically weak.

Each paper and each editor had his own individual story, though, so generalizations are inappropriate. Some, like Sam Brannan, the ex-Mormon who founded *The California Star,* were dynamic and even ruthless. Others, like Edgar Wilson Nye of the Laramie *Boomerang,* were lighthearted humorists. Still others, like Asahel Bush of *The Oregon Statesman,* seemingly dipped their pens in acid.

All of them, in their own way, brought news, entertainment and controversy to the citizenry of the Old West.

There were no schools of journalism as we know them today, so most frontier newsmen had little formal training in their profession. As a matter of fact, many of them had little schooling of any kind. Grammar and spelling errors in weathered old file copies attest to that deficiency. This was no particular drawback, however, because few of the readers were any better off academically.

In the beginning the printer-editor was the rule rather than the exception. A young man who had learned to hand-spike type as a devil "back East" was apt to turn up as the entire editorial staff and production department of some remote village weekly. Sometimes he became a good writer, quite often not.

It was the period of personal journalism, when

Division of Manuscripts, Library, University of Oklahoma

(Above) John P. Clum was a typical frontier editor. At 26 he bought out the *Arizona Citizen* in Tucson, and three years later he launched the famed *Tombstone Epitaph* in a tent-covered shack on May 1, 1880. Before that he had been an Indian agent among the Apaches, and later he served as postmaster and mayor of Tombstone.

In some respects story-tellers and even historians have over-rated the pistol and carbine as standard equipment of frontier journalists—and yet, there were duels and shootings enough to lend credence to their tales. Untempered editorial attacks occasionally found their climax in formal challenge, attacks on the street or ambushes. The sketch at left depicts the killing of Edward Gilbert, editor of the *Alta California,* by General J. W. Denver for whom the Colorado capital was ultimately named. The duel later prevented Denver from becoming a Democratic presidential candidate.

libel laws were rare. Consequently, some editors became well-known, not necessarily because they were gifted writers, but because of the way they lashed out at fellow newsmen and other citizens in bar-room and back-alley terms.

One frontier editor called another "the most unscrupulous liar in the Territory." The other lashed back with "roller boy, slanderer-general and 'pimp' generalissimo." In Kansas, Dan Anthony of the Leavenworth *Times* described rival newspapermen as "three of the lowest, dirtiest, filthiest scoundrels that ever infested any place on earth." In reply, one of them wrote of Anthony that even dogs would pass him by "writhing in agony in search of a cleaner post."

This kind of editorial billingsgate did little to raise the public esteem of newspapermen, but it certainly entertained the populace. It also sold newspapers, which even in those days was a most important consideration.

It will be obvious as this book unfolds that politics played a big role in early-day newspaper-

Controversial but materially successful, William Randolph Hearst, Sr. (left) took over the *San Francisco Examiner* on March 4, 1887, when he was 24 years old. Not a "frontier editor" by any means, Hearst still entered the field in the early stages of Western journalism and started at once to build his gigantic newspaper empire.

(San Francisco Examiner Photo)

(Below) This rare old photo shows William McKay of the *San Francisco Bulletin* covering the Modoc Indian war of 1872-73. While he writes his dispatches on his knee, two Indian riflemen crouch in a lava rock emplacement in the rugged Klamath country of northern California.

This was considered the ultimate in modern news coverage at the Spokane (Wash.) *Spokesman-Review*, circa 1897. The telephone and typewriter, symbols of journalistic speed, were coming into general use, and reporters, using relics like those shown here, were able to get the news quicker and transcribe it more accurately than ever before. After 1874, when E. Remington & Sons began to market an improved version of the Sholes and Glidden typewriter, newsmen could anticipate the end of writer's cramp as an occupational disease.

ing. And vice versa. Editors reveled in it, lambasting the opposition and glorifying the party heroes. Many newsmen became candidates and office-holders themselves, but more often they were the banner-wavers and tossers of the barbed dart.

The great fun of frontier newspapering was that even the smallest towns often had two or more editors to keep the pot boiling as they exchanged invective or goaded one another to editorial combat. Sometimes those battles ended in tar-and-feathers, bullwhippings, bowie knives or bullets.

Not always were the squabbles merely inter-paper affairs. It was not uncommon for infuriated individuals or an occasional mob to get into the act. After printing a particularly inflammatory story, a newspaperman could expect to be accosted on the wooden sidewalks or in the local saloon. Since he was—more often than not—a lone wolf, he could seldom blame the words on someone else.

The editors of the Old West can certainly take their place in history proudly—for not only did they write and print the news of the raucous frontier, they helped make it!

Thomas Wickham Prosch (right) was one of Washington State's leading pioneer publishers. As a young man, he edited and printed Tacoma's first newspaper, the *Daily Pacific Tribune*, on August 9, 1873, after he had moved a press and type cases from Olympia by boat. He later published the *Seattle Post-Intelligencer*.

The *Blair* (Neb.) *Tribune* emerged weekly from this un-imposing one-room plant, which was not unlike hundreds of others throughout the West. The type-slinger perched on his high stool, while Editor Bill Strode presided from his tilt-back chair. The strategically located stove insured survival during prairie winters. (Opposite page) The Division of Manuscripts of the University of Oklahoma Library provided this photo of an unidentified composing room.

A Shirt-Tail Full of Type.

"Half a dozen printers—pale and generally ema-ciated men hurrying toward tuberculosis from bend-ing ten hours a day over dusty cases of type—stood in their alleys . . . a grimy, four-smelling, filthy place it was."
William Allen White
Re: *Emporia Daily News*, (1886)

THE PROBLEMS OF GETTING OUT a frontier newspaper were aggravated by the crudity of the equipment possessed by most West-ern publishers.

The *Idaho World* came into being on a com-posing "stone" fashioned from a planed-down pine log. The chase was made of old horseshoe iron, and a tobacco box tin served as a type-stick.

In Oregon City, George L. Curry printed the *Free Press* in 1848 on a build-it-yourself wooden press with remnants of an old French type font. He supplemented his alphabet with w's hand-carved in hardwood.

The *Cherry Creek Pioneer,* Colorado's second newspaper, was produced on an indestructible old Ramage which had spent several years in the Missouri River where beleaguered Mormons had thrown it to keep it from an angry Gentile mob.

17

Roby Wentz

The composing room of *The San Francisco Chronicle* supposedly looked like this in 1879. Typographers in frock coats set type for the crusading daily which had grown from a give-away theater sheet begun in 1865 by two young brothers, Charles and Michael H. de Young. They called it *The Dramatic Chronicle*, dropping the "Dramatic" three years later when they found themselves with a full-fledged newspaper. Charles de Young was shot and killed in 1880 as the result of an editorial battle. His assassin was the son of a mayoralty candidate whom de Young himself had wounded. This happened about the time the lithographic print shown here was made. All those lamps, incidentally, created more fumes than light.

This is what the well-dressed printer wore when he worked for the Anselmo (Neb.) *Sun*, circa 1890. A composing stick and planing mallet were tools of the trade, and this compositor displays them proudly, along with derby and pipe. The so-called "tramp" printer traveled with little more equipment than his union card—and often he didn't even have that.

Nebraska State Historical Society

Such mechanical handicaps were commonplace to the establishment of the Fourth Estate in the Western wilderness. Largely, it was a problem of transportation which prevented the shipment of equipment and supplies from the East. On the other hand, progress in the development of printing apparatus was slow and relatively unimaginative. Even the best had its drawbacks!

By present standards it didn't take much money or equipment to get into the newspaper business in the small communities of the Old West. An Army press, a bundle of "readyprint" and a "shirt-tail full of type" were the principle ingredients.

The press, of course, created most of the problems of transportation because of bulk and weight. Ultimately there were many kinds and models, but in the beginning, the choice was quite limited. By 1850, however, the Cincinnati Type Foundry—the most notable supplier of frontier printers—was producing the famed Washington hand-press. This marvelous old apparatus

The elimination of the slow and tedious principle of the Gutenberg press was a boon to Western printers. In Philadelphia in the early nineteenth century George Clymer invented the Columbian, a press operated entirely by a series of compound levers. It was a predecessor of the Washington hand-press.

18

—developed in 1827 by Samuel Rust, who later sold the patent to R. Hoe & Co.—became the symbol of "country journalism."

Most early newspapers were "hand-pulled." Because of the poor quality of ink and paper, it was often necessary to dampen the sheets beforehand in order to get a readable impression. This merely added to the difficulties of getting out an edition. Under such circumstances a publisher couldn't have served more than the two or three hundred subscribers if he wanted to.

But the demands for speed, greater circulation and more profit hurried the development of more efficient equipment. About 1832 Robert Hoe made the first cylinder press ever used in America. Before that, steam-driven bed-and-platen presses had been devised for Eastern big-city newspapers, the best of which had been patented by Isaac Adams of Boston.

Various types of steam cylinders followed the hand-presses into the West. They came first to the more populated cities, then spread to the smaller towns as the newspaper business became more and more stabilized.

The local newspaper office was usually the job-printing headquarters for the community, too, so

In time, a version of the Washington hand-press was being manufactured by several printing suppliers. The price list of R. Hoe & Company (above right) shows the the variety of sizes available in the 1890s. (Below) A husband-and-wife team — Mr. and Mrs. Lawrence Crume McShane — "pull" the Hubbard (Ore.) *Chronicle* from an old Washington. (Below right) A nineteenth century job press.

Oregon State Library

R. Hoe & Co.

19

small platen presses supplemented the larger equipment. Business cards, letterheads, bill posters and even books were included among the sometimes crude, sometimes artistic imprints produced in cluttered old shops.

Before the development of practical automatic casting equipment, the type supply on the frontier was also limited. Short fonts and missing letters strained the ingenuity of typographers. The publisher of *The Columbian* in Olympia, Washington, for instance, had just enough display letters to set his nameplate. Then he played a game of anagrams and re-arranged the characters to spell "Notice" with which he headed all job posters.

The lack of type resulted in the dull sameness which characterized many of the earlier Western newspapers. It took an ingenious and completely practical idea to give these little sheets variety—and to solve their paper problems, too.

Ansel Nash Kellogg, publisher of the Baraboo (Wisc.) *Republic,* was one of many who found himself short of help because of enlistments in the Civil War. Unable to gather and set enough material for his paper, he made arrangements

The Cincinnati Type Foundry was established in 1820 (see ad left) by Oliver Wells, a clock-maker. It became a prime supplier of frontier newspaper offices. (Below left) This Hoe cylinder was the first steam press installed in Oregon. It printed the *Oregonian* in 1864. (Below right) Owners of the *Russell* (Kans.) *Record* were proud of this steam-driven patriarch.

Oregonian Photo   The Kansas State Historical Society

CALIFORNIAN.

Vol. I MONTEREY, SATURDAY, SEPTEMBER 5, 1846. No. 4.

THE CALIFORNIAN—Is published every Saturday morning
By COLTON & SEMPLE.
Terms.---Subscription, one year in advance $5 00
"   six months   2 50
Single copies,   12

CALIFORNIA.—No. 3.

From the fact ... ook place at the taking of Sonoma, I feel justified ... the world has not, hitherto, manif. sted so ... ation. The reader will remember that ... onoma, consisted of 33 men, gathered in ... t officers, or the slightest degree of organi... blicly declared object, and each man having ... s ... of the then existing government, and the ... of an ... ncrease of those oppressions, with a clear sense of their danger, their rights, and their duty, they rushed to the rescue with one impulse and one object, the watchword was equal rights and equal laws, and they nobly sustained their principles.

Sonoma was taken without a struggle, in which place was nine pieces of artillery, about 200 stand of small arms, of public property, which was taken possession of. There was also a large amount of private property, and a con-sider-

deportment of the little garrison left at Sonoma, can do them justice, for there has been no time in the hist... the world, where, men without law, without of... t the scratch of a pen, as to the object had ... with that degree of moderation a... persons and property as was ... asion.— Their children, in generati... look back with pleasure, upon th... a revolution carried on by their fath... up ... s high and holy as the laws of eternal ju... e.

A small garrison was left at Sonoma, consisting of about 18 men, under command of Wm B. Ide, which in the course of a few days was increased to about forty. On the 14th day of June, Mr. Ide, by the consent of the garrison, published a proclamation setting forth the objects, for which the party had gathered, and the principle which would be adhered to in the event of their success. The paper itself is plain and concise, and needs no comments of mine to re-commend it.

A PROCLAMATION

To all persons and citizens of the District of Sonoma, requesting them to remain at peace, and follow their rightful occupations without fear of molestation.

(Above) California State Library (Allan R. Ottley)

(Below) Steve L. Watts

One of the legends of early California journalism was that the Bear State's first newspaper was printed with Spanish type which had no w's. A close perusal of early editions proves this to be totally inaccurate. Publishers Colton and Semple simply didn't have *enough* w's, and after running out, they resorted to double v's as indicated in the example above. (Right) This clever bit of prose by a country editor is self-explanatory—and far more truth than fiction.

with David Atwood and Horace E. Rublee of the daily *Wisconsin State Journal* at Madison to provide him with paper printed on one side with war news and other stories which appeared in the *Journal.*

The idea appealed to four other hard-pressed publishers, and soon Atwood and Rublee were offering a similar service to them.

Although there had been abortive attempts at such syndication in the East, this was truly the beginning of "readyprint"—the "patent insides" and "patent outsides"—which played such an important role in early-day journalism. This, at last, was a way for national advertisers to sell their wares through hundreds of small country weeklies.

The "readyprint" business boomed after the war, and A. N. Kellogg became owner of one of the biggest syndicates based in Chicago. Others, like the Western Newspaper Union, entered the field, and a new industry was created.

YE COUNTRY EDITOR ONCE SAID:

*T*HIS *printing business isn't all it's cracqued up to be. We ordered several phonts oph very nice type, but the outphit came without any ephs or cays. This maxes it hard, but we will try to get along as best we can. ☞ We don't lique the loox oph this cind oph spelling any better than you, but mistaques will happen and iph the ph's and c's, and the x's and que's hold out, we shall ceep (sound the 'c' hard) going aphter a phashion till new sorts arrive. It's no joque!*

21

San Francisco Examiner Photo

This was the era of patent medicines—and the "patent insides" sold every imaginable kind of elixir. Kellogg's syndicate alone carried these advertising messages to some 1,400 papers through the medium of half-printed sheets and

several thousand more with stereotyped plates, a service he added in 1875.

The publishers in the field couldn't have been happier. The syndicate offered a paper supply, which a little paper couldn't afford, and interest-

California Department of Parks and Recreation

California's first journal, the *Californian*, was printed on the packing paper from a cigar shipment. That was a far cry from the web rolls being hauled (above) to the *San Francisco Examiner*. During the half-century interim, editors were constantly fearful that the freight wagon with "next week's paper" wouldn't arrive in time. In 1856 Samuel Penfield Taylor erected a paper mill on Daniels Creek north of San Francisco. Rags collected by Chinese in the Bay City were shipped by schooner to Tomales Bay, floated in to Taylor's warehouse at high tide and hauled by oxen to the factory. His second mill (left) was built in 1884; it later burned mysteriously.

Before the turn of the century Linotypes began to come into general use, particularly in the larger metropolitan dailies. The ungodly long hours of hand-spiking needed to produce a single edition were eliminated by these remarkable machines, perfected by Ottmar Mergenthaler and tried out by the New York *Tribune* in 1886. The composing room shown above was that of the Spokane (Wash.) *Spokesman-Review*, circa 1897.

ing features which many unschooled editors were incapable of writing.

Otherwise, frontier newspapermen were ingenious. They had to be! The *Sumner* (Wash.) *News* provides a good example. Anyone who turned over the printer's imposing stone would have read this inscription: "Leroy O., husband of Susan M. Duncan, born May 15, 1811, died May 18, 1865." Leroy O.—whoever he was—gave his all for the cause of journalism.

Gradually, as the West became more populated, the production obstacles were overcome. Inventions like the telephone, the telegraph, the Linotype, engraving processes and many others brought constant change to the industry. In time the rugged frontier editor became a business man—for better or worse!

(Below) This was the historic "blower machine," Ottmar Mergenthaler's original Linotype, which ultimately revolutionized the newspaper business everywhere.

THE WEST'S FIRST LINOTYPES*

State	Paper	City	Date
Arizona	Republican	Phoenix	5-25-95
California	Times	Los Angeles	5-16-93
Colorado	Times	Denver	1-22-92
Idaho	Idaho Statesman	Boise	9-14-98
Kansas	Topeka Capital	Topeka	8-24-94
Montana	Daily Journal	Helena	11-17-91
Nebraska	Omaha Bee	Omaha	1- 8-94
New Mexico	Democrat	Albuquerque	6-17-96
Nevada	Gazette	Reno	2-28-01
North Dakota	Forum & Republican	Fargo	1-28-97
Oklahoma	State Capital	Guthrie	12- 4-97
Oregon	Astorian	Astoria	8-15-92
South Dakota	Pioneer Times	Deadwood	5-16-00
Texas	Post	Houston	3- 1-92
Utah	{ Tribune	Salt Lake City	8-31-93
	{ Herald	Salt Lake City	8-31-93
Washington	Telegraph	Seattle	4-22-93
Wyoming	Cheyenne Sun	Cheyenne	2- 4-93

*Courtesy Mergenthaler Linotype Co.

THE WEEKLY DAKOTIAN.

PUBLISHED BY THE DAKOTIAN PRINTING COMPANY. Where the Flag of our Country Leads, we will Follow. TERMS—$2 A YEAR, INVARIABLY IN ADVANCE.

VOLUME 1. YANCTON, DAKOTA TERRITORY, THURSDAY, JUNE 6, 1861. NUMBER 1.

TO THE AMERICAN FLAG.

When Freedom from her mountain height
Unfurl'd her standard to the air,
She tore the azure robe of night,
And set the stars of glory there!
She mingled with its gorgeous dyes
The milky baldric of the skies,
And striped its pure celestial white
With streakings from the morning light!
Then, from her mansion in the sun,
She call'd her eagle bearer down,
And gave into his mighty hand
The symbol of her chosen land.

Majestic monarch of the cloud
Who rear'st aloft thy regal form,
To hear the tempest trumpings loud,
And see the lightning lances driven,
When strides the warrior of the storm,
And rolls the thunder-drum of heaven!
Child of the sun! to thee 'tis given
To guard the banner of the free—
To hover in the sulphur smoke,
To ward away the battle stroke,
And bid its blendings shine afar,
Like rainbows on the cloud of war,
The harbinger of victory!

Flag of the brave! thy folds shall fly,
The sign of hope and triumph high!
When speaks the signal trumpet's tone,
And the long line comes gleaming on,
Ere yet the life-blood, warm and wet,
Has dimm'd the glistening bayonet,
Each soldier's eye shall brightly turn
To where thy meteor glories burn,
And as his springing steps advance,
Catch war and vengeance from the glance.
When the cannon's mouthings loud
Heave in wild wreaths the battle shroud,
And gory sabres rise and fall
Like shoots of flame on midnight's pall,
Then shall thy meteor glances glow,
And cowering foes shall shrink beneath
Each gallant arm that strikes below
That lovely messenger of death.

Flag of the seas! on ocean wave
Thy stars shall glitter o'er the brave;
When death, careering on the gale,
Sweeps darkly round the bellied sail,
And frighted waves rush wildly back
Before the broadside's reeling rack,
Each dying wanderer of the sea
Shall look at once to heaven and thee,
And smile to see thy splendors fly
In triumph o'er his closing eye.

REPRODUCE HERE THE FIRST ISSUE OF THE PAPER IN LONGEST CONTINUED PUBLICATION IN SOUTH DAKOTA. THE FRONT PAGE CONTAINS THE LAWS OF THE UNITED STATES SETTING UP THE TERRITORY OF DAKOTA AS APPROVED March 2nd 1861.

FROM THE ARCHIVES OF THE SOUTH DAKOTA HISTORICAL SOCIETY.

Cherry Creek Pioneer.

VOL. 1.   DENVER CITY, KANSAS, APRIL 23, 1859.   NO. 1.

THE PIONEER

—Is published—

Every Saturday Morning,
AT DENVER CITY,

Arapahoe county, Kansas.

For the Pioneer.

SONG FOR THE TIMES.

By a Frontier Individual.

Tune–" Har I Times" come again no more.

There's a crowd in every village, and every
town, astir,
Who are going to gather up the gold;
There's a sound in every cottage, and a

bottom land to accommodate all who
will follow agricultural pursuits for
some time to come, and the upper
prairies will be used for stock ran-
ges.

Captains Theodore and William
Parkinson are opening a farm in
the bottom below town, and are
well satisfied with the soil

the opening of spring, expecting men
who have been here during the winter to point them out rich diggings
disappointed in this, they turn back.
They have not stopped to consider
that men who came here as early as
the 1st of last November, had their
cabins to build, and when that was
done winter had set in and although

This is the only edition of the loser in Western journalism's most famous race. It came off the press 20 minutes after the *Rocky Mountain News* had already been proclaimed Denver's first newspaper on April 23, 1859. The next day

John Merrick, the publisher, reputedly sold out to the victor for a grubstake and marched off to seek his fortune in the gold fields. Vol. 1, No. 1 of the *News* is shown on page 60.

Volume 1, Number 1.

"A company incorporated itself and started a paper . . . the paper was published in the loft of a livery stable. This is the reason they called it a stock company."

Bill Nye
Laramie *Boomerang*, 1881

Historians have long sought the evidence to establish conclusively the "first newspaper" in each of the Western States.

It would be a simple matter to determine, if all Vol. 1, No. 1 editions still existed—but fires, carelessness and the ravages of time have done away with the "proof positive" in several cases. In still others, it has been a matter of definition: What constitutes a *real* newspaper?

In Nevada, for instance, the *Territorial Enterprise* has generally been considered the first chronicle in the flamboyant Silver State—but two hand-written "manuscript" papers are known to have preceded it. Were they truly newspapers and entitled to consideration?

The East Bannack News Letter appeared in the old Montana territorial capital almost a year before *The Montana Post* was issued in Virginia

The *San Diego Herald* would have been the first paper in southern California—had not parts of the plant been "lost along the way at the bottom of the Chagres River and in the ashes of the San Francisco fire." As it was, it finally appeared on May 29, 1851, just 12 days after the *Los Angeles Star* made its debut.

City on August 27, 1864. Most researchers say *The Post* deserves the honor, however, because *The News Letter* was just what its name indicated.

A similar circumstance occurred in Kansas where *The Shawanoe (Shawnee) Sun,* an Indian-

THE WASHINGTON GAZETTE.

VOL. 1. SEATTLE, KING COUNTY, W. T., AUGUST 15, 1863. NO. 1.

The Cavalryman's Story.

"Tell again." the grand-ire faltered,
Sitting by the farm-house door,
"Tell again the tale unaltered,

The Question of Endurance.

The following paragraph is from an editorial article in the Raleigh (N. C.) Prog-

immense army-losses by battle and pestilence and fatigue and want have been wholly exhausted by rigorous and all-embracing conscriptions, while, in the loyal States, com-

WHAT HAS BEEN ACCOMPLISHED —The month of July thus far has been a crisis for the Jeff. Davis conspiracy, and a perfect avalanche of victories for the Union. Oter

THE SEATTLE GAZETTE.

VOL. 1. SEATTLE, KING COUNTY, W. T., DECEMBER 10, 1863. NO. 1

THE SEATTLE GAZETTE,
PUBLISHED WEEKLY

By J. R. Watson & Co.,
SEATTLE, W. T.

TERMS:

Per Annum, in advance, · · · · · · $4 00
Six months, " " · · · · · 2 00
Single copies, · · · · · · · · 12¢
Advertisements inserted at the customary rates.

Old Friends.

All gone but you and I, old friend !
All gone but you and I !
What do we here, when in their graves
Our old companions lie ?

dollars means Europe. Two thousand dollars means Egypt, Palestine and Greece.

Boys dealing in small sums reckon the same way. Penny means a stick of candy; sixpence is but another term for ball; shilling means a kite, and fifty cents a jack-knife.

The young "Crack" sees in his money a skeleton wagon, and a fast nag, a rousing trot, a jolly drink, and a smashing party.

But many and many a weary soul sees in every shilling, bread, rent, fuel, clothes. There be thousands who hold on to virtue by hands of dollars; a few more save them; a few less, and they are lost. Their gayer sisters see feathered hats and royal silks in their money, or rather in their fathers' and their husbands'.

The poor scholar passes daily by the stall

From Naples to Rome.

The line from Naples to Rome runs through very beautiful scenery, the long line of the snow-capped Abruzzi bounding the horizon on the east through almost the entire distance. The old Greek costume of the women, (seen at many points, and particularly about Veletri, exactly as it was imported into Italy by the Greek colonies thousands of years ago,) is very picturesque and gay, its bright colors and easy folds seeming quite in harmony with the tone of everything else in the landscapes.

As yet there are only a few huts at the different stations, not even a glass of water being procurable, except at Cepraus, on the frontier, where a wretched attempt at a buffet has just been opened, the viands consist-

WAR NEWS.

Dates to November 26th.

Union Victories at Chattanooga. Lookout Mountain and Missionary Ridge.

WASHINGTON, Nov. 25th.—Official dispatches from Grant and Thomas, at Chatanooga, Nov. 24th, state that on yesterday Palmer, Grant and Harvy's corps charged on the first line of rifle pits between Chatanooga and the creek, and captured nine officers and about 300 men. Our loss was 100.

To-day, Hooker, with Granger's and Osterhaus' divisions, and two brigades of the 4th corps carried the north slope of Lookout Mountain. The enemy's loss is about 600. Our loss is small.

Oregon State Press Association

Special Collections, University of Washington Library

language publication, can be traced to March 1, 1835. The first English-language newspaper—*The Kansas Weekly Herald* of Leavenworth—did not appear until almost two decades later, on September 15, 1854. The question is: Was *The Sun* a newspaper or merely a religious pamphlet of the Baptist Mission?

The biggest argument, though, concerns which early journal was "First in the West." A disputed possessor of the laurels is the *Oregon Spectator,* whose Vol. 1, No. 1 carries the date of February 5, 1846. While the Oregon City paper was obviously first on the coast, other Western gazettes pre-date it considerably.

If you include foreign language papers and pre-territorial journals, Nacogdoches, Texas, would logically be the "birthplace of Western journalism." There, in 1813, Jose Alvarez de Toledo published a revolutionary sheet called *El*

(Above) *The Washington Gazette* was really just the prospectus for *The Seattle Gazette* which followed, yet both carried the Vol. 1, No. 1 designation. The August 15, 1863, prospectus was actually printed in Olympia; the later paper became Seattle's first. The two titles and datelines have created research confusion ever since. (Left) Replicas of the West Coast's first paper—the *Oregon Spectator*—were reproduced for the Oregon State centennial in 1959.

In 1873 Bismarck, Dakota Territory, was a tiny village of 150 cottonwood shacks and tents. To that prairie hamlet — originally known as Edwinton — came 30 - year - old Clement A. Lounsberry, an ex-military officer and a Minneapolis newspaperman.

He brought with him a wagonload of printing equipment and the kind of determination it takes to start a paper where there were no schools, no banks, no organized churches or—for that matter—no roads. The railway had not yet arrived and only 12 homesteads had been filed.

But Lounsberry was gambling on the future of this Missouri River townsite, and his seven - column **Bismarck Tribune** appeared with Vol. 1, No. 1 carrying a dateline of July 11, 1873. Actually, he had planned to publish on Independence Day, but it took longer to set the type than he had estimated, and—so the story goes—he was fearful that his legal advertising, if dated on a holiday, might be invalid.

The Tribune became a daily in 1881, and the next year it carried the words "North Dakota" in its masthead, seven years before the State was actually established. The building on the left was its home in early years. It has been burned out three times in its career, but publication has never ceased.

The Bismarck Tribune (Jack Case)

Mejicano. A second paper—also devoted to ousting the Spanish—was issued by Dr. James Long, last of the filibusterers.

In 1829 Godwin Brown Cotton established his *Gazette* in San Felipe, Texas. In Taos, New Mexico, in 1834, a Spanish-language paper—*El Crepusculo de la Libertad (The Dawn of Liberty)*—struggled through several editions. A year later the *Shawnee Sun* appeared in Kansas. Also preceding the *Spectator* was *The Cherokee Advocate*, a dual-language paper printed at Tahlequah, Indian Territory, in 1844.

The object here is not to complicate the picture

with further arguments for one claimant or the other, but to point up that any controversy reduces itself simply to a matter of interpretation until some dusty attic or archive reveals new facts.

On the following page, the earliest known newspapers in each of the 17 Western States have been compiled in chart form. This listing may well not be the final verdict, but it establishes a jumping-off place for further exploration by other historical sleuths.

It is doubtful that many of the young editors and printers on the edge of the wilderness real-

THE FIRST NEWSPAPERS IN THE OLD WEST

STATE	NEWSPAPER	LOCATION	DATE	PERSONNEL
Arizona	The Weekly Arizonian	Tubac, Terr. of New Mexico	Mar. 3, 1859	Edward E. Cross, Editor
California	Californian	Monterey, Calif. Terr.	Aug. 15, 1846	Rev. Walter Colton, Editor Robert Semple, Printer
Colorado	Rocky Mountain News	Cherry Creek (Auraria), Kans. Terr.	Apr. 23, 1859	William N. Byers, Publisher
Idaho	The Golden Age	Lewiston, Washington Terr.	Aug. 2, 1862	A. S. Gould, Editor
Kansas	The Kansas Weekly Herald[1]	Leavenworth, Kansas Terr.	Sept. 15, 1854	William J. Osborn and William H. Adams, Publishers
Montana	The Montana Post[2]	Virginia City, Montana Terr.	Aug. 27, 1864	John Buchanan, Editor Marion Manners, Printer
Nebraska	Nebraska Palladium and Platte Valley Advocate[3]	Bellevue, Nebraska Terr.	Nov. 15, 1854	Thomas Morton, Publisher
Nevada	Territorial Enterprise[4]	Genoa, Utah Terr.	Dec. 18, 1858	W. L. Jernegan & Alfred James, Publishers
New Mexico	El Crepusculo de la Libertad	Taos, New Mexico (Prov. of Mexico)	1834	Fr. Antonio Martinez[5]
North Dakota	Frontier Scout	Fort Union, Dakota Terr.	July, 1864	Winegar & Goodwin, Publishers
Oklahoma	The Cherokee Advocate[6]	Tahlequah, Indian Terr.	Sept. 26, 1844	William P. Ross, Editor
Oregon	Oregon Spectator	Oregon City (Unorganized Terr.)	Feb. 5, 1846	W. G. T'Vault, Editor John Fleming, Printer
South Dakota	The Dakota Democrat	Sioux Falls City, Nebraska Terr.	Sept. 20, 1858	Samuel J. Albright, Publisher
Texas	El Mejicano[7]	Nacogdoches (Prov. of Spain)	1813	Jose Alvarez de Toledo, Publisher
Utah	Deseret News	Great Salt Lake City, Deseret	June 15, 1850[8]	Dr. Willard Richards, Editor Brigham H. Young, Printer
Washington	The Columbian	Olympia, Oregon Terr.	Sept. 11, 1852	James W. Wiley & Thornton F. McElroy, Publishers
Wyoming	The Daily Telegraph	Fort Bridger, Utah Terr.	1863[9]	Hiram Brundage, Publisher

Notes:

1. The *Shawanoe (Shawnee) Sun*, an Indian-language publication, was first issued at the Baptist Mission in present Johnson County on March 1, 1835.

2. *The East Bannack News Letter*, of which no known copies presently exist, is generally accepted as Montana's first publication, but its qualifications as a true newspaper have been disputed. Some authorities say an earlier news sheet (name unknown) was produced by Wilbur F. Sanders, whose printer's devil was John A. Creighton, who later founded Creighton University at Omaha.

3. Vol. 1, No. 1, July 15, 1854, was printed in St. Mary's, Iowa.

4. At least two manuscript papers—the *Scorpion* and the *Gold Canyon Switch* — preceded it.

5. Some researchers contend that *The Dawn of Liberty* actually was edited by a man named Barreiros.

6. In August of 1844 *The Cherokee Messenger* was issued at the Cherokee Baptist Mission, but it was more of a religious and temperance pamphlet than a newspaper.

7. Other newspapers appeared during the filibuster period, when Texas was under Mexican rule and during the decade of the Republic.

8. According to Mormon history the first paper was printed at 5:20 p.m. the previous day, but the dateline was set to read June 15 instead of 14.

9. Only two issues of this paper have been substantiated, neither of which appears to be the first.

The saga of Sam Brannan is a colorful chapter in California history. Before he was 20, young Brannan had been a newspaper publisher in New Orleans. Several years later he helped establish a Mormon paper in New York City. In 1846 he was put in charge of an L.D.S. colony migrating to California and into the hold of the chartered ship, **Brooklyn,** he stowed a press, type, paper and ink.

The **Brooklyn** arrived at Yerba Buena on July 31, 1846, and immediately Brannan launched into a career as an entrepreneur which soared to great heights and then collapsed disastrously. One of his projects was the establishment of the Bear State's second newspaper, The California Star, on January 9, 1847. His editor was Elbert C. Jones, and Vol. 1, No. 1 explicitly announced that **The Star** would **not** be a Mormon sheet. Brannan and the Church soon parted ways, and he went on to great success and great failure. **The Star** and the **Californian,** the state's first paper, later merged to become the **Alta California.**

ized that they were creating history when they pulled Vol. 1, No. 1 from their inefficient old presses. The excitement of the moment probably precluded any thought of future generations. The 50 or so copies of *El Crepusculo* certainly reduced the odds on preservation. Hiram Brundage's tiny paper at Fort Bridger came and went without a trace of his first issue.

Complicating the picture, too, are the fictionalized versions of historical events, written by the buck-and-byline seekers and given more notoriety than they deserve. Subjects of shallow research, these glamorized stories are merely history-based fairy tales.

The same license has been taken with the frontier editor and printer. The former—if we are to believe the horse-opera scripts—went about trying to prove that the six-gun was mightier than the quill, while the latter were *all* poetic tramps, ruining their eyes and their lungs merely to buy another bottle.

For the story-tellers, the truth is often much too dull!

The paper below is Vol. I, No. 1 of the re-established *Cherokee Advocate,* dated March 1, 1876. Thirty-two years earlier it had been founded at Tahlequah, Indian Territory, and edited by William P. Ross (inset).

THE MONROVIA PLANET

N°5

(Opposite page) *The Monrovia* (Calif.) *Planet* was established in 1886 during the transcontinental railroad "boom." The young newsboys shown here found ready customers for their papers. (Above) The hunger for news was never more dramatically recorded than in this photo taken on June 22, 1898, at Dawson City, Yukon Territory. Seven copies of the *Seattle Post-Intelligencer* arrived that day and were sold for $1.50 each. This audience reportedly paid $1.00 a head to hear one of the lucky purchasers read the story of Schley's victory at Santiago and other news tidbits.

Land Notices and Stomach Bitters.

"The Hon. C. A. Franklin has abandoned his purpose of starting a newspaper in Phoenix and in lieu of that last Saturday started a Faro bank."

Arizona Daily Star
June 3, 1883

NOT THE LEAST INCIDENTAL FACTOR in establishing a frontier newspaper was making it pay.

Early journals had publishers, editors and printers (often the same person filled all three roles), but there was seldom any mention of a business manager. That's why scores of little

papers went broke almost before the ink dried on their first editions.

The around-the-clock problems of news-gathering, typesetting, printing and then distribution of the forms for the next issue were so demanding that there was little time left for the purpose of keeping the wolf from the door.

Files of country papers are filled with editorial appeals for cordwood, potatoes, chickens and other vital commodities which publishers were anxious to receive in exchange for advertising space or subscriptions. The editor of the Flagstaff (Ariz.) *Sun-Democrat* in 1897 wrote:

31

Everything—from stomach bitters to soothsaying—was advertised in the newspapers of the Old West. This assortment came from the Weaverville (Calif.) *Weekly Trinity Journal* (Ye That Suffer and Notice); the Webster (Dak. Terr.) *Reporter and Farmer* (No Brag!); Lindsburg (Kans). *Localist* (Liver Pills); the Atoka (Indian Terr.) *Vindicator* (Opium) and the Fresno (Calif.) *Expositor* (Attention! Sinners!).

". . . we will take money, bonds, bills, notes, cast-off clothing, or anything else animate or inanimate in exchange for our newspaper efforts."

The editor of the Corinne (Utah) *Daily Reporter* felt differently in 1872:

"No barter edvertising for pianos, watches, or sewing machines taken! *Cash only,* and no notice taken of anything else!"

Hard cash was needed, to be sure, to purchase supplies and to obtain the services of itinerant printers. The latter often worked for so-much-per-thousand-ems on a pay-as-you-go basis, and insolvent publishers were partly responsible for their continuing travels in search of a job where the wages came regularly. Some, of course, were simply the victims of wanderlust.

Covering as many years and as much territory as we do in this volume, it is difficult to generalize with any accuracy on facts and figures. But as late as 1895 skilled printers in Kansas were working for $8 a week, women typesetters up to $4 and devils $2.50. Reporters received as much as $10. Supply houses were lenient with credit, although "readyprint" usually came C.O.D. to the express office—where the newspaperman picked it up when he had the cash.

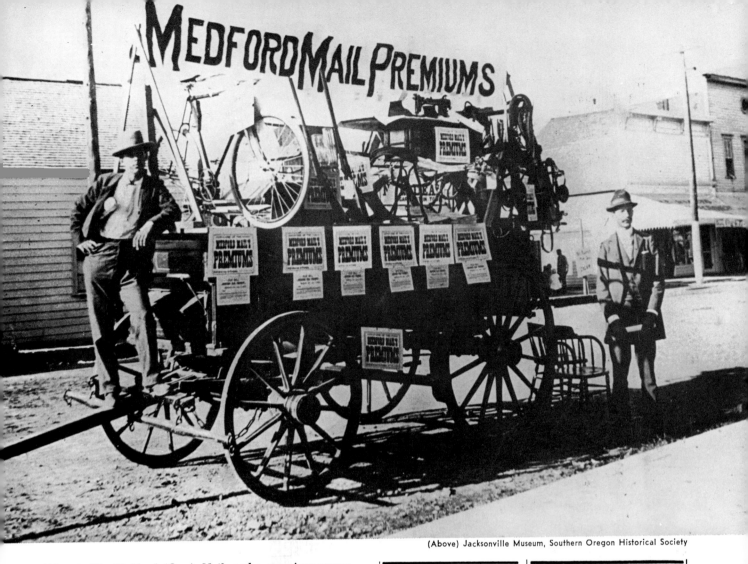

MEDFORD MAIL PREMIUMS

(Above) *The Medford* (Ore.) *Mail* used a premium wagon to drum up subscriptions, a unique and effective promotion. (Below right) Legal advertising kept many small newspapers in business. Land notices to prove up homestead claims were particularly helpful, and in certain areas, brand announcements provided revenue.

Though wages were modest and supplies reasonably cheap, newspapering was not an easy way to make a living, and certainly not the sure road to riches. William Allen White, the famed publisher of the *Emporia Gazette* summed it up this way:

"The editor borrowed with a prodigal hand, built a grand house in the fashionable part of town; and, having passes, he rode up and down the earth, a dashing figure, and mingled with the rich and great in politics. But too frequently the editor was a pasteboard hero, who . . . caved in and went to the scrap heap—a disheveled, vain, discredited old pretender."

Newspaper revenues came from several obvious sources. Subscription sales were important, and

editors pleaded for advance payments of from $1 to $12 or more, depending upon the locale and the period. Display advertising became more and more a factor, first through "readyprint," and then in the individual shops when fancier type faces, sorts, ding-bats and engravings became available. For decades, rates were varied and inconsistent; they were based largely on the principle of what-the-traffic-will-bear.

A continuing lifesaver, however, was the legal advertising. Land and timber notices, required by law to prove up claims, provided a ready source of cash for strategically placed newspapers. As a matter of fact, some greedy young publishers merely followed the homestead trail, producing unimaginative papers crammed with legals on "readyprint" with portable Army presses. They were more interested in the money than journalism, and when the cream was off in one region, they moved on to the next in the vanguard of homesteaders.

When any degree of permanency was achieved,

Job printing was vital to the financial success of most frontier newspapers. The Laramie (Wyo.) *Sentinel* promoted its sideline on its shop front above Pope's Bakery where the aromas of printer's ink and fresh bread intermingled. (Below) Job printing took all forms, from the simplest business cards to health spa and lottery promotions. (Below right) Degener's Liberty Press, one of many types of job presses used in newspaper shops.

Riley County (Kans.) Historical Museum

Washington State Historical Society

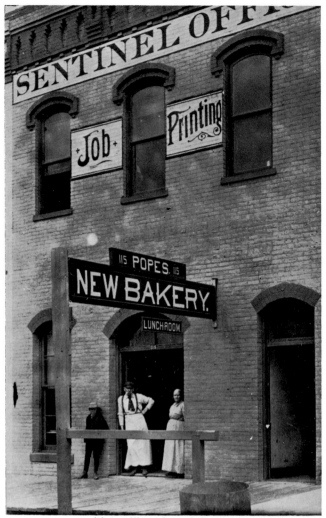

Western History Research Center, University of Wyoming

the newspaper office went into the job-printing business. It provided fill-in work for the printers and revenue to support the entire operation. Quality was often poor, but customers in the small towns either didn't recognize it or they didn't care. They also didn't have anywhere else to turn.

Public printing was usually a profitable plum, and in capital cities and county seats, there was much competition for the awards. It is unquestionable that graft was involved in many instances, as kick-backs and excess charges were all too commonplace. In Washington Territory one Public Printer admitted paying $2,000 to the territorial secretary for the assignment. Later, in the same territory, more than 50 bills were passed by legislators (who had their fingers in the pie) simply to provide public printing jobs. Gov. Alvan Flanders vetoed them all.

Politics brought other revenues to frontier publishers, too. Harry Brook, who published the Quijotoa *Prospector* and worked on other Arizona papers in the 1880s, wrote later:

"An election was harvest time . . . for the publication of a card announcing the candidacy there was a regular graduated rate, running from $10 for a Coroner, to $250 or so for a Sheriff . . . the price charged including a commensurate amount of 'favorable mention'."

One way or another, many of the frontier papers survived and became successful businesses. Along the way, however, there were countless mergers and associations from which developed the hyphenated names of numerous present-day journals. In the process, the pen was important, but the cash register prevailed!

Early newspapers promoted themselves in many ways. They placed ads in various national directories, describing their capabilities and circulation figures. *The Wichita Herald* (below) wanted it known that it was "thoroughly Republi- can." Some papers issued calendars and special editions, and the *Seattle Post-Intelligencer* even had a march dedicated to it. The editors, of course, used news and editorial columns for self-praise.

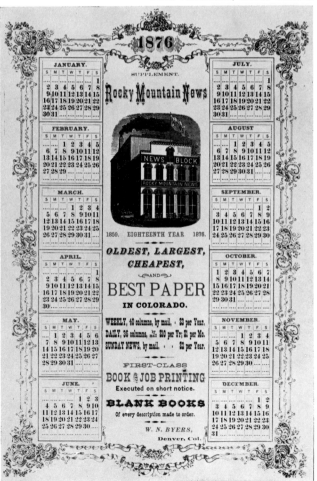

(Opposite page) The Woodward (Okla.) *Dispatch* was one of many non-Indian newspapers which began to appear when western Oklahoma was opened to white settlers. Young newsboys, afoot and on horseback, were an integral part of the scene wherever an old Washington or a "modern" steam press cranked out fresh copies of frontier journals. (Above) *Out West* was Colorado Springs' first newspaper; it later became the *Gazette & Telegraph*.

17 States & 10,000 Gazettes

To TELL THE STORY OF JOURNALISM in the Old West completely, this book would require at least 10,000 chapters.

No one will ever know exactly how many frontier chronicles emerged from the usual admixture of sweat, tears and printer's ink. Yet all of them had their own stories some dramatic, some dull; some a fleeting glimpse and others a century or more of continuing service.

We reiterate that this volume in no way endeavors to trace in detail the history of newspapering in each of the 17 states we've ascribed to the "Old West." Just listing the thousands of tiny papers by name and date would fill these pages. However, our intent has not been to catalog, but to portray graphically—state-by-state—the highlights of a most fascinating segment of Western Americana.

There will be some omissions and a few areas of over-balance, but because this is primarily a pictorial presentation, the availability of photos weighed heavily in the final compilation. From Bellevue, Nebraska, to Monterey, California, then, this is "Newspapering in the Old West."

(Above and Below) Sharlot Hall Historical Museum of Arizona

Arizona:

Varmints, Violence and Vitriol

"Conducting a newspaper in a frontier country is always a perilous, precarious and thankless task."

Edward E. Cross
The Weekly Arizonian, 1859

IN 1897 THE TOMBSTONE *Prospector* had the following to say about frontier journalism:

"Out here in Arizona the life of a newspaper-man is by no means smooth sailing, and those who are looking for a soft snap should choose some other vocation. By devoting the same time, talent, enterprise and brawn to raising peanuts or making adobes, each and every one would secure a better living, and an insurance on their lives would not be classed as extra hazardous."

This, of course, was 38 years after the first newspaper was printed in the territory, and in

(Opposite page) The Tombstone-Bisbee stage attracted this crowd in front of the *Epitaph* and *Prospector* in 1898. The X marks the famed Oriental Gambling House. (Above) Globe, Arizona, was the home of the *Silver Belt,* founded in 1878. (Below right) The *Arizona Democrat* office in Prescott looked like this in 1880.

(Opposite page) Division of Manuscripts, Library, University of Oklahoma

(Above) Originally the *Salt River Herald*, the first paper in the new town of Phoenix, was established in 1878 as a Republican weekly, three years before the city was incorporated. (Below) The *Arizona Enterprise* of Prescott was short-lived. Founded in 1877, it disappeared two years later, right after this picture was taken.

the interim, a lot of flamboyant history was written. The exploits of Wyatt Earp, Billy the Kid and Geronimo were hand-spiked by printer-editors for tiny papers which faced greater odds than did the "Cow Boys" at the OK Corral.

The first press came to Arizona after a long, circuitous journey. It was a trusty Washington, manufactured in Cincinnati and ordered by William Wrightson of the Santa Rita Silver Mining Company. From Ohio, it was barged down river to New Orleans, sent by ship around the Horn to Guaymas, and then hauled overland by ox cart to Tubac. The latter city, along with Tucson, was a Mexican presidio before the Gadsden Purchase. When the press arrived early in 1859, Tubac had about 400 inhabitants—most of them Mexicans and Indians. It was a most unlikely place to publish a successful paper.

But on March 3 of that year, Editor Edward E. Cross produced the first issue of *The Weekly Arizonian*. In a matter of weeks he was engaged in a controversy with Lt. Sylvester Mowry, an ex-

The *Arizona Star* started life in Tucson as *The Daily Bulletin* on March 1, 1877. Before the end of the month, its name was changed and it continued as a tri-weekly. Under its new title, its proprietor was Louis C. Hughes, destined to be territorial governor and first president of the Arizona Press Association in 1891.

Arizona Pioneers' Historical Society

army officer who had been elected a delegate to Congress for the proposed Territory of Arizona. Cross opposed territorial status, and he wrote that Mowry had lied about the region's population figures. The West Pointer promptly challenged the editor to a duel in which no one was injured, though each fired two shots at 40 paces with Burnside rifles. Both, incidentally, were still in their 20's. Mowry then bought the press and moved *The Arizonian* to Tucson. The original peripatetic Washington produced the paper until 1868 when it was replaced by a newer model. It was not retired, however, being used to print the first issues of the *Arizona Citizen* (see opposite title page) and the *Arizona Star* (right) in Tucson, after which it turned up in Tombstone in January of 1879 to produce *The Nugget,* first newspaper in that booming silver town. All of which brings us to the next rollicking phase of Arizona journalism.

In 1878 a roving prospector named Ed Schieffelin located the fabulous "Loma de Plata" (Hill of Silver) northeast of Fort Huachaca. The secret slipped out, and a silver rush was on. Be- low the slopes, a settlement of shacks and tents was officially christened "Tombstone" by the miners. By 1880 the boom town boasted two thousand citizens; two years later that figure was multiplied by five. Already two newspapers were on the scene: the aforementioned *Nugget* and a daily with a most appropriate name, the *Tomb-*

stone Epitaph. The latter's 29-year-old editor, John P. Clum, named it himself because, as he later wrote, "every Tombstone needs an epitaph."

(Above) A Civil War correspondent for the *New York Evening Post,* Richard C. McCormick came west to establish the *Arizona Miner* at Fort Whipple in 1864. It was moved

Clum (see page 13), who had previously owned the *Arizona Citizen* in Tucson, was lured to the burgeoning mining camp. With his printing

to Prescott after the sixth edition. The *Miner* gained prominence after 1867 under the editorship of vitriolic John Marion. (Below) Backshop of the Prescott *Prospect.*

Arizona State Department of Library and Archives

(Above) The *Epitaph* office in later years. (Below) An example of the *Epitaph's* inside typography in 1890.

equipment due any day from San Francisco, he finally appealed to busy workmen who erected a 20x40 foot wooden framework for him. In Tucson he bought canvas enough to cover the top, and under those unpretentious circumstances, the *Epitaph* was born.

Few Old West newspapers have received as much notoriety as the *Epitaph* (Clum himself had said that the name would be worth a million dollars in publicity). Few newspapers also were located in the midst of so much excitement! It chronicled the boom-to-bust era, and then lingered on as subterranean water drowned out the once bountiful silver mines.

Titles like the *Nugget, Pick and Drill, Prospector, Our Mineral Wealth, Bullion* and *Arizona Miner* pointed up the importance of gold and silver in the territory's economy. In Prescott, the *Miner* was a particularly well-read and much-quoted newspaper. One of its early editors, John H. Marion, was a poignant, often biting writer who played the game of personal journalism full-hilt. His editorial battles with Judge William J. Berry of the Yuma *Sentinel* were classics in libel

TOMBSTONE EPITAPH.

PUBLISHED EVERY MORNING

(MONDAYS EXCEPTED)

BY

MEEK & MADERO.

Fourth Street, between Fremont and Allen Tombstone, Cochise County, Arizona.

ENTERED IN THE POST OFFICE AS SECOND-CLASS MATTER.

TERRITORIAL REPUBLICAN TICKET.

Election Tuesday, November 4, 1890.

For Delegate to Congress:
GEO. W. CHEYNEY, OF COCHISE.

Joint Councilman, Southern District:
W. F. NICHOLS, OF COCHISE.

Joint Councilman, Northern District:
J. M. W. MOORE, OF YAVAPAI.

COUNTY REPUBLICAN TICKET.

TERRITORIAL COUNCIL.
R V. VICKERS .... Tombstone
TERRITORIAL ASSEMBLY
HOWARD F. HERRING.. Tombstone
WM. HUGHES .... Bisbee
GEO. F. MEEK............ Tombstone
H. C. HERRICK............ Fairbank
L. V. WILKINSON........... Benson
SHERIFF.
CHAS. OVERLOCK .. Sulphur Spring
TREASURER.
J. P. McALLISTER....... Tombstone
RECORDER.
W. F. BRADLEY .... Tombstone
ASSESSOR.
N. A. GILMAN............ Willcox
DISTRICT ATTORNEY.
GEO. W. SWAIN.......... Tombstone
PROBATE JUDGE.
F. N. WOLCOTT........... Tombstone
SURVEYOR.
C. L. BECKWITH .... Bisbee
SUPERVISORS.
D. H. LOGAN .... Benson
B F. BROWN............... Bisbee

UNDERTAKERS ASSOCIATION

Pioneer Establishment.

(Ritter Building)

ALLEN STREET, OPPOSITE O. K. CORRAL

FRARY & Co., Managers.

The largest and finest stock of Undertaking Goods in Arizona. We are prepared to do all work in our line in a first class manner. ALL OUR WORK GUARANTEED.

Bodies Embalmed

Or temporarily preserved in a trifling expense for shipment.

Satisfaction Given in All Respects.

☞ Orders left at the O. K. Stable will receive prompt attention.

ALLEN WALKER, FUNERAL DIRECTOR.

El Diario del Hogar, a paper of the City of Mexico, asserts that the Mexican navy consists of only five ships, the Independencia, Libertad, Xicotencatl, Colon and Democrata. The paper also says that in case of war none of the above-mentioned vessels will be useful. Nevertheless Mexico has a navy that can be utilized in times of peace, and the paper then naively adds: "We are coming up to the English navy."

A prominent physician and old army surgeon in eastern Iowa was called away from home for a few days; during his absence one of his little children contracted a severe cold and his wife bought a bottle of Chamberlain's Cough Remedy for it. They were so much pleased with the remedy that they afterwards used several bottles at various times. He said, from his experience with it, he regarded it as the most reliable preparation in use for colds, and that it came the nearest being a specific of any medicine he had ever seen. For sale by H. J. Peto, Druggist.

62,480 540

Is the Total Population of the United States.

AN AWFUL CASE OF POVERTY

Wholesale Arrests in the Postoffice Department of San Francisco— Mexican Duty on Cattle

Only Fifty.

ZANZIBAR, Nov. 1.—An official report states that the British loss is fifty killed and many wounded.

Gone Back.

NEW YORK, Nov. 1.—The Compte de Paris and suite sailed for Liverpool to-day.

Defeated.

SYDNEY, Nov. 1.—In the legislative assembly a motion expressing a want of confidence in the ministry was defeated by a vote of 46 to 22.

The Colorado and Midland Sold.

TOPEKA, Nov. 1.—The stockholders' meeting of the A. T. and S. F. railroad to-day ratified the purchase of the Colorado and Midland. No other business was transacted.

Killed for Ten Cents.

SAN FRANCISCO, Nov. 1. — John Brown, waiter in the Excelsior restaurant, was stabbed and killed by F. C. Beck, in a quarrel in a saloon over a ten-cent drink, about 2 o'clock this morning. Beck was arrested.

Stopped Some of Them.

BERLIN, Nov. 1.—The "Vossiche Zeitung confirms the report from Warsaw that a number of persons who were leaving Russia for Brazil, were fired upon by a Russian frontier guard at Slupca. The Warsaw report stated that nine were killed, but the Zeitung says four.

43

and invective. Their feud was carried on weekly and was avidly followed by readers in both towns.

Of Berry, Marion wrote: ". . . his first great care was to fill himself with whiskey, after which it was his custom to walk, like the swine that he is, on all fours to his den."

In kind, Judge Berry penned: ". . . we had the extreme mortification of seeing the editor of the *Miner* . . . laid out in the refreshment room, dead drunk, with candles placed at his head and feet, and a regular 'wake' held over him. It was then for the first time that we discovered Darwin's connecting link between the fish and the quadruped. As he lay, with the drunken slobber issuing from his immense mouth, which extends from ear to ear, and his ears reaching up so high, everyone present was forcibly impressed with the fact that there was a connecting link between the catfish and the jackass."

No question about it, early Arizona journalism was exciting and bombastic. Each frontier gazette had its own story and, altogether, these tales added up to a vital chapter in the saga of the Old West!

(Left) John H. Marion, the outspoken editor of the *Arizona Miner*. (Below) The first Territorial Press Association of Arizona met in Phoenix in 1890. Louis C. Hughes, front row center, editor and publisher of the *Arizona Star*, was elected president. He later became territorial governor and chancellor of the University of Arizona.

Both pictures: Arizona Pioneers' Historical Society (Nova M. Alderson)

Backshops of the *Arizona Citizen* (above) and the *Arizona Star* (below), both of Tucson. Note that each made considerable use of women typesetters, including a lady Linotype operator. The two papers dated back to the 1870s when Tucson was the territorial capital. Both survived an era when dozens of tiny journals failed.

California:

Gold Bullion and Type Metal

"We have received two late numbers of the Californian, a dim, dirty little paper . . . published and edited . . . by a lying sycophant and . . . an overgrown lickspittle."

The California Star
San Francisco, 1847

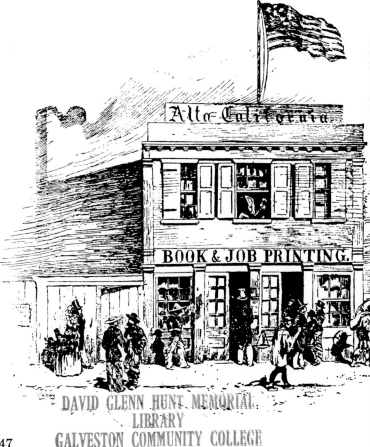

THE MASS MIGRATIONS TO CALIFORNIA —especially after James Wilson Marshall made his dramatic discovery at Sutter's Mill in 1848—brought almost immediate demands for news. Gold on the frontier seemingly had a great affinity for type metal, and where the former was found, the latter appeared soon after.

In California, however, newspapers preceded

(Opposite page) Fires were disastrous to many early newspapers. The San Francisco *Daily Morning Call* was ravaged in 1859. (Above) First newspaper in the goldfields was the *Sonora Herald*, printed on the old *Californian* press on July 4, 1850. (Right) The *Alta California* grew out of the *Californian* and The *California Star*.

(Below) Bancroft Library, University of California

(Above) Visalia Times-Delta Photo

A MEMENTO

Charles de Young

FOUNDER OF THE

SAN FRANCISCO CHRONICLE

ASSASSINATED APRIL 23, 1880

the gold. At Monterey in 1846 Rev. Walter Colton, a chaplain from the U.S. frigate *Congress*, found the old wooden-frame Ramage which had been discarded by the Mexican provincial government. With it were several handsful of badly worn type and part of a keg of ink.

In the meantime, Colton had become acquainted with a giant Kentuckian named Robert Semple, whom he described as "true with his rifle, ready with his pen and quick at the type-case." Together they re-conditioned the old material, cut rules and "leads" from sheet-tin with a jack knife and on August 15 issued the state's first newspaper: the *Californian* (see page 21).

Several months later in San Francisco (then Yerba Buena) Sam Brannan, the ambitious, recalcitrant Mormon elder, followed with his *California Star* (see page 29), printed on an acorn-model

(Above) The *Tulare Times* was established on June 12, 1865. In later years it merged to become the *Visalia Times-Delta*. (Left) Charles de Young and his brother were teen-agers when they first published *The Dramatic Chronicle* as a theater news-sheet in San Francisco on January 16, 1865. Three years later it became *The Daily Morning Chronicle*. Charles de Young was shot and killed in 1880 by the son of the notorious Rev. Isaac S. Kalloch. Earlier de Young had wounded the minister as the result of a political dispute involving the Workingmen's Party.

48

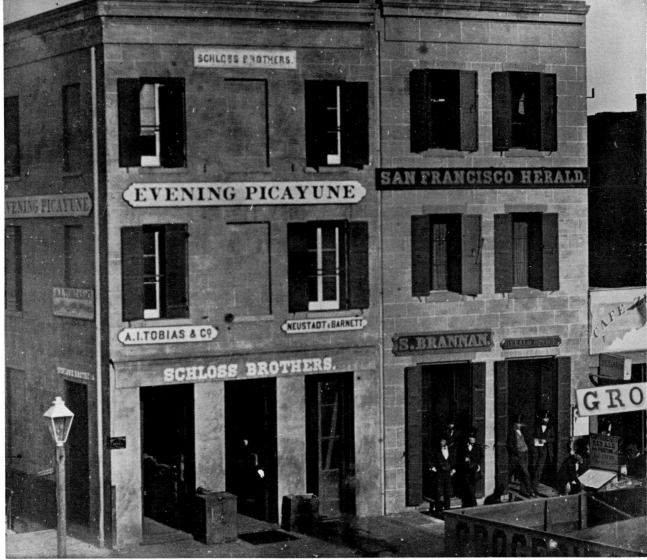

(Below) Denver Public Library Western Collection

(Above) Bancroft Library, University of California

Washington hand-press. From the beginning he was competing with the *Californian* which had moved up from Monterey—and yet both papers missed the big story of the age!

It was weeks before either of them even mentioned James Marshall's discovery, and when they got around to discussing gold, they attacked the rush to the Mother Lode country as "all sham—a superb take-in." In a matter of days, however, both papers suspended publication because all the printers had departed for the gold fields, too.

When the initial excitement of the gold boom subsided, Edward C. Kemble—who had been an

(Above) Two short-term San Francisco papers—the *Evening Picayune* and the *Herald*—were both founded in 1850. Note the office of Sam Brannan, the dynamic entrepreneur, in the *Herald* building. (Left) One of the most noted early California editors was James King of William, whose slashing editorials in the *Daily Evening Bulletin* resulted in his murder by political boss James P. Casey in 1856. Casey was hanged by vigilantes, and King's funeral procession was routed past the dangling body.

49

(Above and below) Historical Collections, Security First National Bank

The Los Angeles *Daily Times* made its first appearance in 1881 but was soon taken over by the *Weekly Mirror* (above), founded eight years earlier. Water power from the city ditch operated the press which occasionally stopped when fish clogged the intake pape. Col. Harrison Gray Otis combined the two papers to form the *Times* in August of 1882. (Below) The second home of the *Times* was dynamited in 1910 as the result of a 20-year labor dispute.

editor for Sam Brannan—merged *The Star* and the *Californian* on November 18, 1848. Soon after, it was re-named the *Alta California,* and as such, it became one of the Bay City's most influential papers.

Meanwhile, the discovery of gold and the influx of new settlers were catalysts in the expansion of the Fourth Estate. The *Californian's* doddering Ramage traveled up river to New Helvetia (Sacramento) where it produced the *Placer Times* under Editor Kemble's direction. From there the same press was shipped to the tent-city of Stockton. There its ancient platen squeezed out the first issue of the *Stockton Times and Tuolumne City Intelligencer.* While in the same location, it also printed Vol. 1, No. 1 of the *Sonora Herald,*

the Mother Lode's first journal. Later the press was transported to Sonora and then to gold-rich Columbia where it turned out the *Star.* This was the end of the road for the much-traveled patriarch. Known by scholars as the Zamorano Press (for Agustin V. Zamorano, the Mexican official who originally ordered the press from Boston), the tired Ramage was destroyed by vandals in Columbia following a dispute over payments.

By the end of 1860 California had about 100 newspapers, of which 40 were in San Francisco. The latter figure included 14 dailies. With so much competition, it is no wonder that the journalistic graveyard was a busy place. This was the era of the Vigilance Committees, when private citizens banded together against lawlessness.

The *Visalia Weekly Delta* in Tulare County was typical of many early California papers. In 1888 the staff below produced the *Delta* in what was once an old church. Newspapering in Visalia was particularly volatile during the

Civil War when the *Delta* lost an editor in a gun battle, and a rival sheet—the "Copperhead" *Equal Rights Expositor*—was ransacked by irate Union soldiers from nearby Camp Babbitt.

Illustrated editions made their appearance early in California as evidenced by the Christmas number of *The Pictorial Union* shown above. Other stock cuts—like the "laughing boy" in the *Mayfield Palo Alto*—showed up later in many country weeklies. (Below) Among the luminaries of early

California journalism was Bret Harte. At 21 he served as a compositor and writer for the *Northern Californian* in Uniontown (Arcata). Later he became editor of a literary magazine, the *Californian,* for which he accepted numerous editorial contributions from a contemporary, Mark Twain.

James King of William, the editor with the euphonious name, militantly committed his *Bulletin* to the vigilantes' cause. His paper out-stripped all others in the city, but in the end he was murdered by political boss James P. Casey, who was hanged in turn by the committee.

Following the vigilante period, the next era of violence in which newspapers participated was the Civil War. Gold had brought many Southern sympathizers to California, and when secession was imminent, tempers flared as far west as the Pacific. A number of "Copperhead" newspapers were established, and bitter editorial taunts soon erupted into mob action.

The pro-Confederate *Democratic Press* of San Francisco was one of the leading "secesh" papers, and as an aftermath of President Lincoln's assassination, Unionists wrecked the plant and threw its type out the window. Captain William Moss, the founder, had to change the paper's name to the *Daily Examiner* before he could reopen with any degree of safety. It was this property which

George Hearst ultimately bought in 1880 to lay the foundation for a great family newspaper tradition.

Meanwhile, Lincoln's death played an important role in the development of another small journal. Charles and Michael Henry de Young, 19 and 17 respectively, had—on January 16, 1865—begun publication of a theater house bill they called *The Dramatic Chronicle.* In spite of cramped quarters, the youthful publishers offered a desk to a correspondent of the *Carson City* (Nev.) *Appeal* named Mark Twain.

The Dramatic Chronicle was just three months old—without a telegraph service and not yet a full-fledged newspaper—when the news of Lincoln's murder reached San Francisco. It came via a Western Union bulletin which was posted at 8 a.m. The morning papers were already on the street without a word of the tragedy, but the resourceful teen-agers copied the telegram and rushed through an extra. From that moment, the paper was destined for a whole new journalistic career.

While the gazettes of San Francisco and the

(Right) William Randolph Hearst, Sr., in his late twenties, shortly after he assumed control of the *San Francisco Examiner* in 1887. (Below) Part of the editorial department of the *Examiner* before the turn of the century.

San Francisco Examiner Photos

"Before" and "after" pictures of the *San Francisco Examiner*. The building below was destroyed by earthquake and fire in April, 1906. The paper was produced in "temporary" quarters (above) until a new home was built.

Mother Lode country were blossoming like spring flowers, another chapter in California's newspaper history was beginning in the south. In 1850 Los Angeles was a small town, with a non-Indian population of about 1,500. In March of 1851 several San Francisco papers ran a prospectus, promising a dual-language paper for Los Angeles the following month. When *La Estrella de Los Angeles (The Star)* finally appeared—almost six weeks late on May 17—it brought journalism to a once-sleepy pueblo, rapidly becoming a rip-snorting frontier town.

With the gold rush to the north creating an insatiable demand for cattle from the south, Los Angeles began to grow. So did lawlessness. The *Alta California* called the southern city "a rendezvous for villains," and soon *The Star* was advocating vigilantism. Meanwhile, the small paper kept itself solvent by winning a state contract to print laws in Spanish. This subsidy lasted long enough to get it past the toddling stage. Not only did it survive money problems, but it licked the paper shortage, too. Transportation from San Francisco was so slow that news arrived as much as seven weeks late, and newsprint even later. Finally, on October 16, 1852, the editor wrote confidently: "It is indeed refreshing . . . to look upon a bundle of good white paper, and to feel an assurance that we shall not again be compelled to resort to brown paper, nor blue paper, nor cigar paper."

After the first newspaper came to San Diego in 1851, a flurry of publications followed in ensuing decades. *The Daily Bee* (above) and *The Daily & Weekly Sun* (below) were among the early chronicles in an era of hopeful development. Mergers were common and mortality high as publishers jockeyed to stay in business.

The Star got local competition in 1854 with the advent of the *Southern Californian*. With a touch of biting humor, the latter lost no time in attacking its rival's professionalism. It editorialized: ". . . in our first numbers, we took some pains to publish our thoughts in bad English, knowing that the public had become familiar with *The Star* readings, and not wishing to make the change too radical for their convenience."

For a time both papers published Spanish sections, but in 1855 Francisco P. Ramírez, the 17-year-old editor of *The Star's* Spanish pages, started his own paper: *El Clamor Público*. For more than four years it remained the primary journal for the "native Californians."

Farther south, J. Judson Ames, a 30-year-old giant who had once killed a man with his bare

fists, brought newspapering to San Diego on May 29, 1851, with his *Herald* (see page 25). Previously he had edited the *Dime Catcher* in New Orleans, but when the gold boom hit in California, he headed westward with his Washington handpress. While Judge Ames was a fiery editor until he died of apoplexy at 40, his greatest act in journalism was to go away and leave his paper in

Two *Bees* buzzed in different parts of California during the late 1800s. (Above) The *San Diego Daily Bee* as it appeared in 1887. (Below) In Sacramento, the *Daily & Weekly Bee* spent almost a half century in this building after it was founded on February 3, 1857. Under the editorship of James McClatchy, the *Bee* was anything but a drone. As the emphasis shifted from gold to agriculture, the paper battled the powerful cattle and mining interests and won both battles in behalf of the small farmers in the Sacramento Valley. It was also involved in railroad squabbles. (Below left) *The San Francisco Examiner's* photo engraving department, circa 1900.

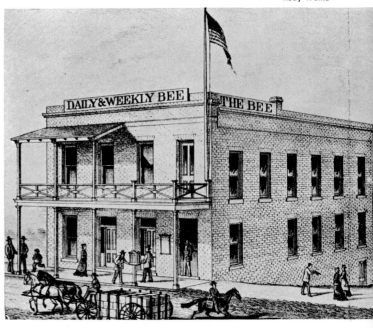

(Above) The back shop of the *National City News*, a latter-day community weekly in San Diego. (Below) Established as a daily in 1868, *The San Diego Union* was another of that city's numerous papers.

the pixie-like hands of Lt. George H. Derby for several weeks. As "John Phoenix," Derby turned the paper into a giant farce, even going so far as to oppose the gubernatorial candidate Ames had left to support. An irrepressible wag, Derby had been assigned by the army to dam the San Diego River—but he found greater sport "damning it" in the columns of the *Herald*.

So it was that the Fourth Estate in California got off to a kaleidoscopic start with humor, with violence, with wealth and deprivation, with vigilantes and Copperheads. The alloy created of gold and type metal proved an exciting mixture!

In its hey-day, Columbia in the Mother Lode country boasted 143 faro games, 30 saloons and an arena for bull-and-bear fights. During its wild history, 10 newspapers came and went, including the *Columbia Gazette*, shown here. It was also in Columbia that the famous Zamorano press was finally destroyed by vandals in 1851.

The Cripple Creek gold rush rekindled the excitement of earlier boom periods in Colorado as miners and opportunists flocked to the new region in 1892. *The Crusher* brought news to the wealth-seekers, and in keeping with the spirit of the occasion and the locale, the editor had the first edition printed in gold ink.

Colorado:

Horace Greeley's West

". . . newspapers, like toads shut up in a dark cellar, are characterized by a wonderful amount of vitality, and live upon nothing for an almost incredible period."

Western Mountaineer
Golden, Colorado Territory

T HE STORY OF NEWSPAPERING in Colorado starts with a great race. It is spiced with kidnappings, gunfire, pilfered presses, the drinking proclivities of Eugene Field and the promotional schemes of Horace Greeley.

The Pikes Peak Gold Rush of 1859, which ended in such bitter disappointment for the "gobacks" who failed to find their fortunes, left instead a ramshackle cluster of huts and leantos on Cherry Creek which would one day grow into a major metropolis.

Known by such names as Montana City, St.

(Above) The *Rocky Mountain News,* winner of a dramatic race against time, became Denver's first newspaper. This sketch depicts the activity involved in getting out an edition. The weapons are prominent because during this period Editor Byers was feuding with some of the lawless element of the rowdy town. (Below) "Uncle Dick" Wootton's saloon and store in Auraria as conceived by an artist for *Frank Leslie's Illustrated Newspaper.* The *News* was first printed in its attic.

State Historical Society of Colorado

(Above) The first issue of the *Rocky Mountain News*. Note in the dateline that Cherry Creek was still in Kansas Territory at the time. The inset shows William N. Byers, the publisher (right rear) following a buffalo hunt with some cronies. (Below) The *News* moved into this log cabin in Auraria in December of 1859. The cabin, which also served as a jail and stable, was more substantial than Wootton's attic.

Denver Public Library Western Collection

Charles, Auraria and Denver City, the tiny settlement escaped a ghost-town demise when John H. Gregory discovered a rich vein of gold-bearing quartz near what is now Central City. The Gregory Lode started the fever all over again, and this time it wasn't a flash-in-the-pan. But the Big Race wasn't to the gold fields!

Unknowingly at first, John L. Merrick and William Newton Byers became the contenders in a dramatic episode which is unique in Western journalistic history. With the first inkling of gold finds along Little Dry Creek in 1858, Merrick had purchased an historic old press in St. Joseph. It had been fished out of the Missouri where it had been thrown when an angry mob destroyed a Mormon printshop in Independence. Merrick loaded the rehabilitated equipment into a covered wagon and headed westward toward the gold country.

Meanwhile, Byers, an Omaha real estate man, decided about the same time that a newspaper in

the Pikes Peak vicinity would be a good investment. He and his associates found a complete printing outfit available in Bellevue, site of Nebraska's first paper, and promptly made arrangements to move it by wagon train to the new Eldorado.

Merrick arrived on Cherry Creek four days earlier than Byers, but not anticipating any competition, he made preparations for his newspaper without haste.

Byers, on the other hand, moved rapidly and made arrangements to house his equipment in an attic of a crude store building belonging to R. L. (Uncle Dick) Wootton. Almost immediately the settlers sensed the impending contest at the type cases, and soon both crude printshops were caught up in the excitement of the race to publish the first paper in the new region.

Bets were placed, and miners and other townspeople moved back and forth between the two shops, cheering the printers on. Unfortunately, the typographers were already working under conditions far from ideal. Quarters were cramped, lighting was poor and sleet had begun to fall.

Byers and his crew were supposed to be in

(Above) Not the wisest thing William Byers ever did was to house his young *Rocky Mountain News* in a creek bed. A flash flood in 1864 swept away the building, a new steam press and the older equipment he had brought so laboriously from Nebraska. His press was found in 1899, buried in the sand of Cherry Creek. (Below) While *The News* had been demolished, the rival *Commonwealth* across the creek in Auraria had survived. Simeon Whiteley offered his paper's editorial columns to Byers, who quickly accepted the neighborly gesture.

Wood sidewalks and hitching posts were part of the scene in the hey-day of the country weekly. Typical was the Canon City (Colo.) *Mercury* (above) as it appeared in 1884. (Below) Few frontier shops could match the neatness of this one. A composing room with flowers was unheard of—but not at the Georgetown (Colo.) *Courier*. Generally the shops were ink-spattered and knee-deep in paper. The time pressures of the business didn't allow much opportunity for housekeeping—and most of the early newsmen didn't seem to mind.

the best building in town, but the roof leaked so badly that a canvas had to be stretched over the top of the Washington hand-press to keep it from getting soaked. Undoubtedly, Merrick and his helpers found their problems equally as exasperating.

Finally, with a giant Negro named Jack Smith operating the lever, Byers' press produced the first copy of the *Rocky Mountain News* on Saturday evening, April 23, 1859. Just 20 minutes later, Merrick had the first copy of the *Cherry Creek Pioneer* on the street. It was a night of great significance in little Denver City, and the citizens made the most of it.

With the decision obvious, John Merrick sold his well-traveled little Ramage for a purported $30 to Tom Gibson, one of Byers' associates. Merrick then hiked off in search of gold, and the tiny press went on to serve other papers in Colorado and New Mexico.

Byers, meanwhile, found himself involved in another competition. This time it was between the ambitious villages of Auraria and Denver City lying on either side of Cherry Creek. The publisher, in what he thought was a Solomon-like maneuver, moved his equipment into a building which was virtually astride the stream bed. That way, Byers figured, he couldn't be accused of showing favoritism to either side. His strategy backfired, however, when a disastrous flood on May 20, 1864, washed building and all away. His press wasn't found until 35 years later.

Before the flood, Byers had an even greater scare. After a scathing editorial attack on the notorious Criterion saloon, the editor was kidnapped by a gang of desperadoes who made the establishment its headquarters. The saloon-keeper —a lodge-brother—helped Byers escape, and he barricaded himself in his printshop to await the inevitable.

Finally, an especially vicious character named George Steele made a one-man assault on the *News* office. Jack Merrick, then back on Byers' payroll as a printer, let Steele have a blast of buckshot. Before any further attacks could be made, a posse of decent citizens intervened, killing Steele and banishing the lawless element.

Newspapering was thus off to an auspicious start in the region destined to become the Centennial State. The first expansion, of course, was in the surrounding mining camps.

The wandering Mormon press which John Merrick had brought from St. Joseph played a star-

The Denver Post

The Denver Post (above) had a rather inauspicious beginning. It was founded on August 8, 1892, and the first issue was published in the basement of the old Curtis Theater. It supported Grover Cleveland, who was very unpopular in Colorado, and the paper folded, largely as the result of the stand. It tried again in 1894 and barely survived the depression, finally being sold to Frederick G. Bonfils and Harry H. Tammen, who turned it into a dynamic newspaper. (Below) The Montrose (Colo.) *Messenger* was founded in 1882, six years before this photo was taken. Such papers usually had two or three young helpers.

Denver Public Library Western Collection

Newspaper offices were popular hangouts in many Western communities, and in 1882 the Gunnison (Colo.)

Denver Public Library Western Collection

Review was no exception. Note the emphasis placed on job printing on the giant-sized sandwich board.

ring role in the continuing history of Colorado journalism. Tom Gibson, who had bought the press from Merrick, took it to Mountain City, one of the camps along Gregory Gulch, where he issued the *Rocky Mountain Gold Reporter and Mountain City Herald* on August 6, 1859. Heavy snows drove Gibson and many of the miners out of the Gulch, and with them went the press. George West, a young printer, bought it and took it to Golden where, on December 4, he published the *Western Mountaineer*. Of the four papers started in the region during 1859, one press had squeezed out three of them.

And still it was not ready for pasture. George West joined the army, and the press departed for Canon City. After printing the short-lived

---

Like Mark Train in Nevada and Bill Nye in Wyoming, Eugene Field was a Western editor who went on to greater things in the literary world. From 1881 to 1883 Field was managing editor of the *Denver Tribune* which he brightened with his wit and acrid pen. He himself classified the somewhat maudlin children's verse he wrote in those days as "popular but rotten." Following are two brief essays which appeared in "The Tribune Primer" and which are appropos of newspapering in the 1880s:

The Bottle

This is a Bottle. What is in the Bottle? Very bad Whisky. It has been Sent to the Local Editor. He did not Buy it. If he had Bought it, the Whiskey would have been Poorer than it is. Little Children, you Must never Drink Bad Whisky.

The City Editor

Here we Have a City Editor. He is Talking with the Foreman. He is saying he will have a Full Paper in the Morning. The Foreman is Smiling Sadly. Maybe he is Thinking the Paper will have a Full City Editor before Morning.

David F. Day, a Medal of Honor winner for heroism at Vicksburg, later became known as the "Old Verbal Volcano of Durango." After the war, Day lost his grocery business in Missouri, and with five children to support, he decided to head westward and make a new start. He was cutting cord wood in the mining town of Ouray in southwestern Colorado when a lawyer friend, Gerald Letcher, suggested that they start a newspaper. Letcher scraped up the money, and Day walked 28 miles to Lake City to buy a small printing plant. The first issue of their paper came out on Sept. 5, 1879— and the most unique feature was its name.

Day had said he wanted to put out a paper which was "solid and honest," and he wanted the title to indicate those characteristics. Day was an admirer of an Irish fight promoter in New York named William Muldoon, who had the attributes the new editor championed, so the paper officially became **The Solid Muldoon.**

Day became internationally known as a "paragrapher." Later the paper was moved to Durango, and the volatile editor had the distinction of having 42 libel suits pending at the same time.

Denver Public Library Western Collection

Times, it was shifted to a boisterous camp called Buckskin Joe to produce another *Western Mountaineer.* After a brief rest, the prolific old relic was again carted over the hills to Valmont (also known as Bugtown). D. G. Scouten cranked out the *Valmont Bulletin* with it. At that time, a fierce competition for the county seat was being waged among Bugtown, Burlington and Boulder —and the former had the only paper. Boulder had a prospective editor, but no press, and in the spring of 1867 when Scouten visited that town—probably to sell subscriptions—he was well plied with liquid refreshments. As the local story goes, the Valmont editor was soon in a deep sleep, whereupon a group of Boulder citizens hitched up a wagon, drove to the neighboring town and confiscated the press, the imposing stone and two stands of type cases. It was one of several instances of "press-napping" in frontier journalism. After Scouten revived, he supposedly accepted the coup, and soon the new

Boulder Valley News appeared. The old Mormon press had done it again. The tireless machine later was taken to Elizabethtown, New Mexico, to start a newspaper there.

Meanwhile, other equipment began to find its way into Colorado, and in 1870, when railroad connections were established between Cheyenne and Denver, the period of news-isolation came to an end. All the problems were not solved immediately, however. Like most of the other Western publishers, the Colorado newspapermen operated in constant fear that the next shipment of newsprint wouldn't arrive. The situation became so critical that a paper mill was established at Golden in the winter of 1868-69. At first the plant made only crude brown wrapping paper— but it was good enough in publishing emergencies. By 1871 the Golden Paper Mill was producing newsprint, and the future of newspapering looked brighter.

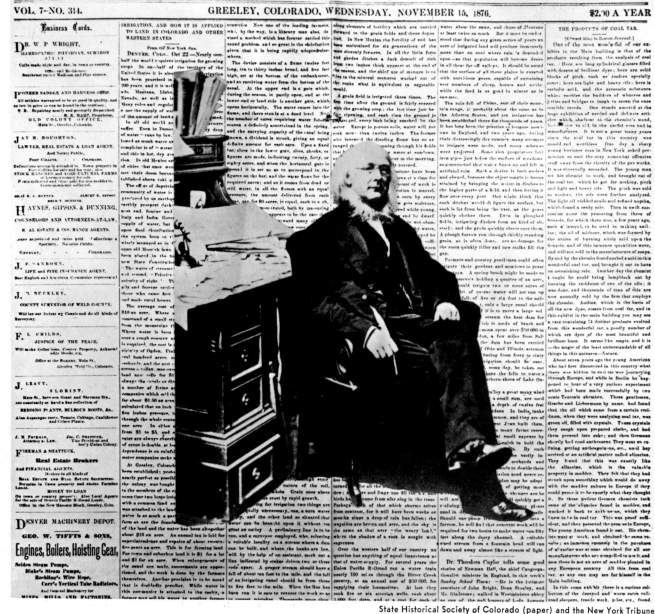

State Historical Society of Colorado (paper) and the New York Tribune

Horace Greeley, the famed editor of the **New York Tribune**, became personally involved in the early development of Colorado. In 1859 when he heeded his own advice to go West, he visited the diggings at Gregory Gulch. Earlier exaggerated reports of gold discoveries had created considerable bitterness among disappointed argonauts who called the venture the "Pikes Peak Hoax." But John Gregory's strike was a rich one, and Greeley's dispatches stimulated a new rush to the region. Local lore has it that Greeley actually was led to a placer which had been "salted" with a shotgun full of gold dust. Obviously he was amazed when he washed a pan of gravel sparkling with color, and he wrote accordingly.

Greeley's other contribution to the area was the Union Colony, a cooperative enterprise conceived and named by the New York journalist. Nathan C. Meeker, the **Tribune's** agricultural editor, headed a party of 50 families to the flatlands in the South Platte Valley. It was an experiment in organized temperance, and one of the "commandments" of the group was "Thou shalt not sell liquid damnation within the lines of Union Colony." During the first year of the new town Meeker established **The Greeley Tribune**. The paper's nameplate was written in Greeley's own hand, reputedly one of the worst in newspaperdom. Typesetters and President Lincoln alike claimed it was unreadable.

Colorado editors, like other Western compatriots, indulged in the raw wit and bitter thrust of personal journalism. Talented writers like Dave Day of *The Solid Muldoon* and Eugene Field of the *Denver Tribune* did more than hurl invectives, however. Day's paper, according to old-timers, was "snatched hot from the press and read amid roars of laughter" by the rugged miners of the San Juan district. The *Tribune* editor, meanwhile, had a continual "Field day" with his barbed banter. As a literary device, Field created the "Colorado cockroach," an emaciated insect which had forsaken the inhumane offices of the *Rocky Mountain News* to grow fat and sleek on editorial paste and soiled towels at the *Tribune* . . . where Field himself kept a row of red ink bottles on his desk—filled with whisky, not ink!

By 1880 newspapering was well established throughout Colorado. That year Carlyle Channing Davis of Leadville had a New York plant

(Above) The stereotype department of *The Denver Post* circa 1901. (Below) This was the home of the *Denver Tribune* just before Eugene Field joined the paper as managing editor in 1881. A bank shared the structure.

The Denver Post

print 60,000 copies of his *Carbonate Weekly Chronicle* on fine calendar paper. He sold the special New Year's edition for 50 cents each; later he bought out six competing papers. His slogan somehow fit the spirit of frontier publishing: "I did unto others what they would have done unto me—only I did it fust!"

That's the way it was in the early days of Colorado journalism—rough, tough and independent. Jesse Randall, who published the Georgetown *Courier,* exposed some political shennanigans and in the election of 1880 got the entire slate of Democrats elected. The rival Republicans vowed to run Randall out of the country and even fired a few cannon balls through the *Courier* front window. The artillery attack failed, but it dramatized the fact that frontier editors had to be ready for most anything!

(Opposite page) Southern Colorado lagged behind the Denver area in the establishment of newspapers. *The Colorado Chieftain* made its debut in Pueblo on June 1, 1868, being founded by Dr. Michael Beshoar and Sam McBride. Judge Wilbur Fisk Stone, shown in hunting garb, was *The Chieftain's* first editor. He lived in the house next to the newspaper office which was in the small building at the left.

(Opposite page) State Historical Society of Colorado

(Above) Composing room of *The Denver Post* near the turn of the century. (Below) Harry H. Tammen, ex-bartender and curio shop operator, and Fred G. Bonfils, son of a Missouri judge and conductor of lotteries, made a most unique combination in the annals of Colorado journalism. They bought *The Post,* then three years old, in 1895, and introduced an era of no-holds-barred newspapering. Libel suits and sensationalism were the order of the day. Once the paper was even sacked by a mob. Nerve center of the operation was the "Red Room," a gaudy office with scarlet walls. To Denverites, it became known as "The Bucket of Blood," and both Tammen and Bonfils were wounded there by gun-fire.

The Denver Post

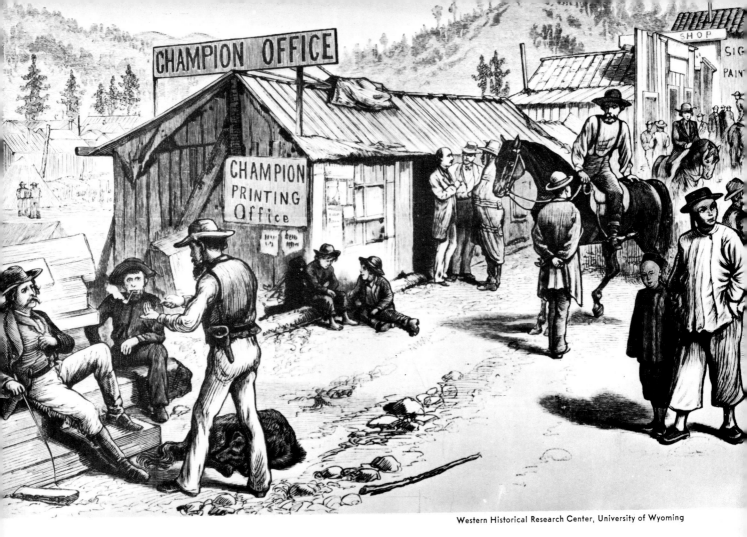

The Dakotas:

Green Prairies and Black Hills

"The average length of a farmer's life is sixty-five years, while that of a printer is thirty-three, hence the necessity of paying for your paper promptly."

The Dakota Republican
Vermillion, Dakota Terr.

FRONTIER NEWSPAPERING IN THE Dakotas developed in two distinct patterns. The settlements on the prairies, along the railroads and in the fertile river valleys soon attracted printers and publishers who wanted "their town" to grow faster than the next one. This was the genesis of the "boomer" spirit which characterized many early newspapers in areas where railroads and the Homestead Act played such major roles.

Meanwhile, the discovery of gold on French Creek near Custer in 1874 set the stage for the last great gold rush in the continental United States—and, of course, created the inevitable

(Opposite page) Deadwood Pioneer-Times Camille Yuill)

(Opposite page) Newspapering in the Black Hills was comparatively "modern" when this picture was taken at the *Deadwood Pioneer-Times*. Steam presses were a far cry from the hand-operated model with which the original *Pioneer* brought the news to Deadwood Gulch in 1876. (Above) The *Black Hills Champion* first appeared in Deadwood City, D.T., on June 2, 1877. This sketch was made for *Frank Leslie's Illustrated Weekly* after owner Charles Collins moved his journal to Central City. (Below) When Sioux Falls City was ransacked during the Indian uprising of 1862, the plant of Dakota's first paper *(The Democrat)* was destroyed. The type was carried away by the Indians who used it to decorate peace pipes. One of the rare lead-inlaid pipes is shown here.

(Above) *The Standard* at Vermillion, D.T., was one of the victims of the disastrous 1881 flood of the Missouri River. Huge ice jams forced the river out of its banks and onto the countryside. The whole town of Vermillion moved to higher ground after the flood. (Below) "Boomer" posters were common in the early days of settlement. This one served double duty as it supported Pierre over Huron as the state capital site.

A Little Baby

ONE YEAR OLD, THIS IS

South Dakota

Huron says this Baby never will grow any larger ; that in twenty years it will be still a little sick baby

"On the Town"

From this she argues that as

HURON IS SICK

The two ought to go together and Huron be the Capital.

Pierre says South Dakota is a Lusty Yearling Baby.

And in twenty years will astonish the world. She has EVERY RESOURCE necessary to make ALL HER PEOPLE RICH. She has the greatest artesian basin in the world, extending from Minnesota to Wyoming and within a short time this country will be covered with artesian wells at the

Expense of the United States Government

FREE TO SETTLERS.

She has the unrivaled agricultural resources east of the Missouri River and

NO POOR SOIL!

The country west of the Missouri River is yet but little understood and has been constantly slandered for a purpose. THERE ARE NO POOR LANDS! IT IS WELL WATERED! It is suitable either for AGRICULTURE OR STOCK RAISING! It is covered over its entire area with the richest grass in great variety. Natural hay is abundant and of all crops the hay crop is the most valuable of the United States, and of nearly every state. Running streams, more abundant than any other part of the West, as follows:

Grand River, 200 Miles Long. Moreau River, 300 Miles Long. Cheyenne River, 300 Miles Long. Bad River, 120 Miles Long. White River, 200 Miles Long.

And over 200 creeks, many of them furnishing fine water powers. It will be seen from the above that Western South Dakota is the best watered country in the west. The water is pure and sweet.

Stop and think what this country of 37,000 square miles will be twenty years hence, and sit down on all idiots who tell you that South Dakota has stopped growing. Now add to the above

THE BLACK HILLS COUNTRY

THE MARVEL OF THE UNITED STATES

robust, ribald and raucous mining camps so common to the wild-and-woolly west.

The development of journalism in the two Dakotas was quite similar. Most of the activity began after the Homestead Law went into effect on January 1, 1863. Thousands of "honyockers" flocked onto the barren prairies to participate in the Great Gamble aptly described this way: "The government bets you 160 acres of land against $18.00 that you will starve to death before you live on it five years." The Homestead Law brought the sodbusters, and right behind them came printers, presses and type cases.

There were pre-Homestead Law papers, however. The first journal was printed at Sioux Falls City even before the Dakota Territory was established on March 2, 1861. That paper was the *Dakota Democrat,* a semi-occasional publication edited by Samuel J. Albright and produced on an old Smith Company press. The first number appeared on July 2, 1859. When Albright left town with the nameplate, the paper continued irregularly as *The (Northwestern) Independent.* It was still in business in 1862 when the Santee Sioux went on the war-path and descended upon the little village. The residents had been forewarned, so they escaped to the stockade at Yankton. But the old Smith press was pitched into the

Theodore Rathjen Collection

Big Sioux River, and the type metal was hauled off by the Indians. Later the type was melted down and used to make inlaid decorations on red-stone peace pipes.

Yankton (originally spelled Yancton) had a pre-territorial paper, too. It was *The Weekly Dakotian,* published by Frank M. Ziebach and William Freney. Volume 1, Number 1 was dated June 6, 1861. Through mergers and expansion, the paper ultimately became the *Yankton Daily Press and Dakotian* (later spelled *Dakotan*), the first daily in the territory—and today the oldest continuously published paper in the "Twin States."

In 1863, when the Homestead "boom" started, newspapers blossomed with each new settlement. Unfortunately, many of these first publications were not established because of the great desires of the editors to bring news and editorial leadership. The prime motive too often was simply Cold Hard Cash. One of the requirements of the Homestead Law was the advertising of "proving up" notices, and opportunists made the most of it. During the hey-day of land development, some so-called "newspapers" carried as many as 200 such legal notices—and at $5 or $6 each, that meant plenty of profit for the publisher.

Yankton Press and Dakotan (Colin Monfore)

(Above) Yankton—"Mother City of the Dakotas"—looked like this in 1861. Its first paper, *The Weekly Dakotian* (below) was printed in the two-story log structure at left in the sketch, after which the press was moved across the street to the building marked "Printing Office." (Right) Two of Yankton's 16 newspapers were printed in this old plant.

The winter of 1880-81 was one of the most bitter in the recorded history of the Dakotas. Heavy snows began to fall in October, and from then until April much of the territory was virtually cut off from the rest of the nation. Mitchell, as a notable example, went 16 weeks without a train. Newspapers suffered most severely from the lack of paper, but because of legal necessity, they had to keep printing. Editors searched out every possible substance on which to publish. Wall paper became the most common substitute and numerous journals (like **The Moody County Enterprise** at right) took on a gaudy appearance. **The Salem Register** of May 20, 1881, was even printed on the design side. Earlier it had been printed on white muslin. Cloth also was used by other editors. The **Egan Express, Mitchell Capital** and **Volga Gazette** were among those printed on various types of wrapping paper. The **Dell Rapids Exponent** appeared on a 9x12 inch sheet of book paper. In the spring the mountains of snow caused new problems as floods wreaked havoc with farms, towns and newspaper plants.

State Historical Society of Wisconsin

(Below) A meeting of the North Dakota Editorial Association at Devils Lake in 1895.

State Historical Society of North Dakota

Needless to say, there was little space to devote to news, and press runs were held to a minimum. Both North and South Dakota witnessed this journalistic phenomenon (as did other states), but somehow after the "easy pickin's" had been harvested, the Homestead hacks disappeared and the legitimate, serious-minded editors began to bring a new brand of newspaper to the permanent settlements. In the spring of 1883, the editor of the *Deuel County Herald* of Goodwin made this forthright comment: "No more land notices for us. We have made an independent fortune and are retiring, stepping out to give another person a chance."

The "boomer" activity marked another phase of Dakota journalism. Railroads constantly promoted the future greatness of prairie towns. The battles for county seats and the two state capitals spurred inter-city rivalries. Towns which no longer exist were boosted as potential Chicagos of the Plains. The desire to be "bigger and better than the other guy" reflected itself in the newspapers of the day as editors dug deeply into their bag of adjectives to lure immigrants and Easterners.

The importance of having a newspaper in a frontier town was well recognized. Territorial Fargo, for instance, was a major outfitting point

(Above) Editor J. E. Britton of *The Courant* in Bottineau, North Dakota, had his home next door to his newspaper plant. (Below) Peering through *The Hunter* (N.D.) *Herald* is Editor Roy F. Porte.

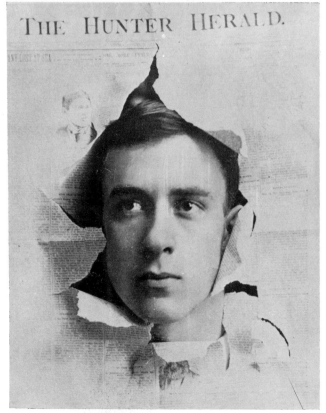

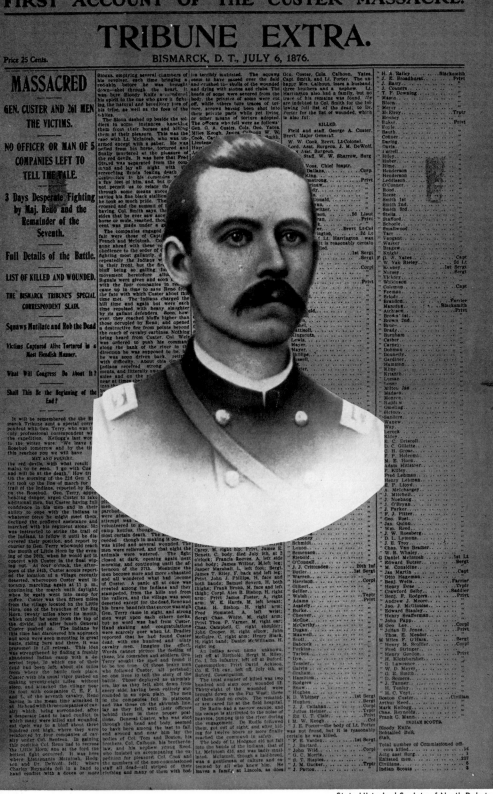

One of the great news stories of the Old West occurred on June 25, 1876, with the tragic defeat of General Custer at Little Big Horn. The world knew nothing of the disaster until the river steamer **Far West** complete a 54-hour dash to Bismarck with the awesome details. On hand to meet the ship was Col. Clement A. Lounsberry (inset left), publisher of **The Bismarck Tribune**. After the initial shock, Lounsberry dashed to the depot where he instructed John M. Carnahan, the telegrapher, to clear the wire to St. Paul. Then he started to write a report of the battle as he had gathered it from returnees on the ship. For 24 hours he wrote while Carnahan and his relief tapped out the news. The story has it that when Lounsberry fell behind, he tossed a copy of the New Testament to the operator and told him to send that just to keep the wire open. Altogether 50,000 words were sent to the **New York Herald** at a wire cost of $3,000. Lounsberry himself received $2,500 for the story. Killed with Custer was Mark Kellogg, a young reporter who went along as a special correspondent.

State Historical Society of North Dakota

The Bismarck Tribune

for settlers heading westward out of Minnesota. It had been named for William G. Fargo, a director of the Northern Pacific Railway and founder of the Wells-Fargo Express Company. Fargo himself offered $500 as a premium for the establishment of a newspaper to be called the *Express*. In June of 1873 two sly operators tried to collect the prize by printing such a paper in Glyndon, Minnesota, but their plot was discovered and the money withheld. On January 1, 1874, a legitimate *Fargo Express* was published, and the bonus paid.

Newspapering in what is now North Dakota actually had its start a decade earlier at Fort Union near the Montana border. The *Frontier*

Scout, a small three-column journal for the troops of Company I, 30th Wisconsin Volunteers, was first issued in July of 1864.

In 1872 Camp Greeley was established at "The Crossing" on the Missouri to protect railroad crews. Where the tracks were to span the river, a small settlement called Edwinton (later Bismarck) began to grow. There, on July 11, 1873, Col. Clement A. Lounsberry established *The Tribune,* North Dakota's oldest continuous chronicle (see page 27). Bismarck and Yankton ultimately fought it out for the territorial capital, and in 1883 the North Dakota city won. Six years later statehood separated the two Dakotas— and an unidentified newspaper played a unique role in the momentous event.

When President Benjamin Harrison was about to sign the proclamations which would admit the 39th and 40th states to the Union, his secretary placed both documents under a newspaper. He then shuffled them back and forth until no one present could tell which was which. Just enough of the proclamations was exposed for the President to sign—and again the papers were shuffled.

(Above) Backshop of the *Larimore* (N.D.) *Pioneer.* (Below) *The Herald* was preceded in Grand Forks by *The Plaindealer.* The two fought bitterly, but when the latter burned out, *The Herald* offered to share its equipment. *The Plaindealer* accepted with thanks—but the editorial battle went on until the papers merged.

No one will ever know which of the two states was admitted first as the result of this historical pea-and-walnut-shell game which occurred on November 2, 1889. By then literally hundreds of newspapers had come and gone in the two new states. When President Harrison signed the proclamations, South Dakota had 275 gazettes and North Dakota 125.

In the meantime, the exciting chapter of journalism in the Black Hills was being written by scores of hardy printers and editors who had been lured by the gold finds of '74. The Hills were actually in Indian Territory until two years later, so the early prospectors were on the scene illegally—and so were the first newspapermen. W. A. Laughlin and A. W. Merrick, who came from Denver with their printing equipment, issued the first number of their *Black Hills Pioneer* on June 8, 1876, almost four months before the Indians ceded the Black Hills to the United States. Between Cheyenne and Ft. Laramie, one of their wagons had tipped over and pied type and equipment. Laughlin became too sick to work, and when they set up shop in Deadwood, it was in an unfinished cabin with an

(Above) *The De Smet* (S.D.) *News* had a float in the traditional Old Settlers' Day parade in 1900. Publisher Carter P. Sherwood worked in shirt sleeves. (Below) The De Smet paper was known as the *News & Leader* when this picture was taken in 1892. Standing in the doorway with Publisher Sherwood was Carrie Ingalls, a pioneer Dakota printer.

Newspapering in the Black Hills area was similar to the exciting brand of journalism which developed in the mining camps around Denver. In fact the first two papers in the Hills had Denver origins. W. A. Laughlin and A. W. Merrick made a winter-time trip to the new Eldorado to establish the **Black Hills Pioneer.** On the way one of their wagons over-turned and Laughlin became desperately ill with arthritis and tuberculosis. When they arrived in Custer, they were "dead broke." Capt. C. V. Gardner, a former Iowa newspaperman, helped raise the $205 they needed to move their gear to Deadwood. The second paper in the historic city was the **Black Hills Times** (right) which was started on April 7, 1877, by Porter Warner, who followed Laughlin and Merrick from Denver. The booming region soon attracted other publishers, among them being Charles Collins, who also had his troubles enroute from Yankton. A fire on the steamer **Carroll** destroyed his press near Fort Randall. He located enough equipment, however, to get out the first edition of his **Black Hills Champion** on June 2, 1877. Collins later moved to Brule City where the fiery publisher established **The Times** and attempted to build a great Irish colony on the prairies. His "army"—which never materialized—was going to invade Canada and drive the British from the American continent.

earthen floor which turned to mud as rain poured through the roof. The press they kept in a tent on a hillside.

After this difficult beginning, the Black Hills became a mecca for journalists. Some tiny mining camps had as many as four papers going at once; in the Deadwood area there were no less than a dozen. As a result compositors were at a premium, and one brilliant publisher solved his typesetting problem this way: On Saturday night, he took his type cases and editorial copy into downtown Deadwood where all the printers came to celebrate. Then he would stage a typesetting contest, offering a couple of bottles of whiskey to the winner. When the competition was over, he had the type for his next edition all ready for the press!

It took such ingenuity to survive in the newspaper business on the frontier. Dakota editors seldom had it easy. The *Douglas County Chronicle* was printed in a calf shed; the *Giles City Chieftain* "went to bed" in a sod shanty, the only building in the "city." In spite of these early draw-backs, journalism persisted, and neither blizzard, flood, fire nor Indian attack failed to dim the light of the Fourth Estate on flatlands or amid gold-laden hills!

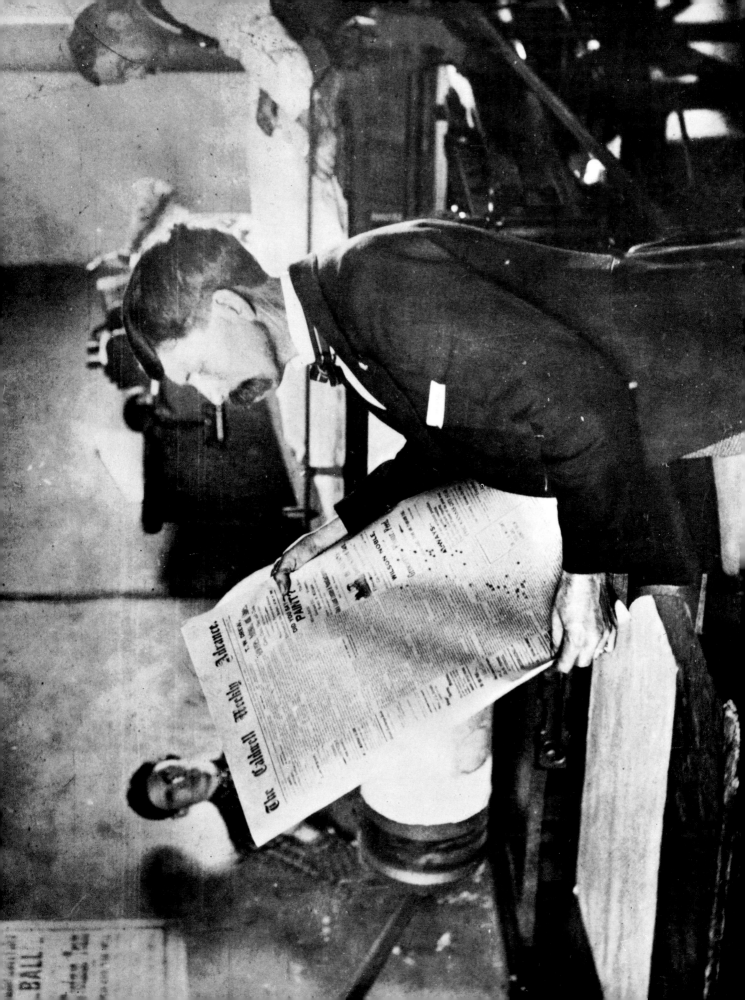

Kansas:

From Dodge City to Potato Hill

"Embry, who shot Anthony, editor of the Leavenworth Times, has been acquitted. That's just the way with some juries—they think it no more harm to shoot an editor than a Jack-rabbit."

Marion County Record
Marion, Kans., 1876.

THE KANSAS-NEBRASKA ACT of 1854 brought journalism to "bleeding Kansas." In granting self-determination to the citizens of the new territory on the question of slavery, Congress had planted some bitter seeds of strife.

"Border ruffians" and anti-slavery Jayhawker guerillas engaged in a vicious struggle which, in retrospect, was a curtain raiser to the Civil War. Into the territory came rabid Free-Staters and Pro-Slavery fanatics. From the beginning newspapers were aligned on either side in the Great Controversy, and printing plants were destroyed

(Opposite page) Editor C. B. McDonald proudly peruses the first issue of *The Caldwell* (Kans.) *Weekly Advance*. (Above) Printing has been taught at Kansas State University since 1873. These students became editors and printers throughout the West. (Below) The *Shawnee Sun* first appeared on February 24, 1835. It was produced by Jotham Meeker, a printer-minister, at the Shawnee Indian Mission near present-day Kansas City.

Kansas newspapers—like other western gazettes—grew from humble beginnings. A great number of them started as family-operated, hand-press ventures like the *Cheney Sentinel* (above). Facilities were varied and often crude. The *Thomas County Cat* at Colby was published in a sod hut (left), while the *Republican Valley Empire* of Clyde had a log cabin home in 1869.

and editors beaten as an inflamed frontier populace was carried away on the wings of emotion.

The Pro-Slavery element got a journalistic jump on the opposition when the *Kansas Weekly Herald* was established "under a tree" at Leavenworth on September 15, 1854. But the Free-Staters were not far behind. While William H. Adams was printing the Leavenworth *Herald* before he had an office, the anti-slavery forces were producing a rival paper—the *Herald of Freedom*—out of the territory. Its first number established as its location "Wakarusa, Kansas"— but Wakarusa was merely a creek on which no town materialized. Its second and later editions were printed and dated at Lawrence.

Other papers were soon espousing one side of the burning question or the other. Southern sympathizers propounded their theories via the *Squatter Sovereign* at Atchison and the *Union* at Lecompton. With backing from out of the

While the *Shawnee Sun* preceded it by almost 20 years, the *Kansas Weekly Herald* is generally considered to be the first regular newspaper published in the state. The *Sun* was an Indian-language publication, and much of its content was devoted to the aims of the Baptist Mission.

The *Weekly Herald* came into being as a Pro-Slavery paper while the first citizens of Leavenworth were still staking out lots. Type for Volume 1, Number 1 was set under a tree. Later the equipment was moved into the first house erected in the new town.

Territory, Free-State journals sprang up everywhere.

The combination of the volatile issue and the rip-snorting "personal journalism" of the era resulted in scathing editorial attacks. These were further spurred by the animosities which developed during the ensuing fight over a constitution. The short-lived Lecompton Constitution—which would have made Kansas a slave state—brought forth livid villification. Sol Miller, editor of the Free-State *Kansas Chief* at White Cloud, blasted a fellow editor who was a delegate to the Lecompton convention: ". . . when the editor of the *Constitutionalist* (Thomas J. Key of Doniphan) came into the world, there was a double birth; one was a baby, and the other a calf—the baby died shortly afterwards!"

For more than a decade the conflict went on, bursting into violence on numerous occasions. On May 21, 1856, Lawrence was sacked by a Pro-Slavery mob, and the equipment of the *Herald of Freedom* ended up in the Kaw River. Josiah Miller's *Kansas Free State* was also the victim of the Lecompton marauders.

During the Civil War itself, the notorious raid by William C. Quantrill brought further destruction to Lawrence. Approximately 200 buildings were destroyed and 10 citizens killed. Amongst the smoldering ruins on that fateful August 21, 1863, was the Lawrence *Republican*.

(Left) The Hiawatha (Kans.) *Dispatch* used this old cut to emphasize collections in 1873. (Right) After the Civil War the number of papers in Kansas increased considerably. Among the post-war journals was the *Republican Valley Empire* at Concordia.

Emporia Gazette Photo

Most famous of Kansas journalists was William Allen White. The editor of the **Emporia Gazette** became internationally prominent as a writer and political king-maker, yet he remained always the small-town newspaper man "with both feet firmly planted in the grass roots."

One of White's best known editorials was one he published on August 20, 1896, entitled: "What's the Matter with Kansas?" It was an angry blast at the Populists, the whiners, do-nothings and the pitiable candidates proposed to represent the state. He wrote: "We have raked the ash-heap of human failure in the state and have found an old hoop skirt of a man who has failed as a business man, who has failed as an editor, who has failed as a preacher, and we are going to run him for congressman-at-large. . . . Then for fear some hint that the state has become respectable might percolate through the civilized portions of the nation, we have decided to send three or four harpies out lecturing, telling the people that Kansas is raising hell and letting corn go to the weeds."

White's editorial was echoed throughout the nation and became a Republican war-cry, not because of what it said about Kansas, but because of its basic philosophies.

This was the baptism which caused newspapering in Kansas to mature rapidly and to assume political leadership. Kansas newspapermen entered the political arena, not only as editorial participants, but as candidates and standard-bearers.

While journalism in the Sunflower State came of age in the period of conflict over the slavery question, there was an earlier chapter of a much different nature. It started with Jotham Meeker, a Baptist missionary who was both a minister and a printer. In 1834 Meeker brought a small press to the Shawnee Mission in northeast Johnson County. There he and Johnston Lykins began to publish the *Siwinowe Kesibwi (Shawnee*

Sun), a small four-page pamphlet which first appeared on February 24, 1835. According to Meeker's diary, he had started to set type for the issue six days earlier. It was an Indian language publication, printed in the orthography Meeker himself had developed. Researchers still argue whether or not the *Sun* could justifiably be called a true newspaper, but semantics aside, the tiny journal appeared well ahead of the English papers and therefore deserves an honored niche in Kansas journalism history.

Following the Civil War, the role of the press on the Kansas prairies changed to conform more closely with that of other western states. It followed the pattern of railroad development and

84

As the state capital, Topeka became an important news-paper city. The top picture is of the composing room of Frank P. McLennan's Topeka *State Journal*. Below is the newsroom of the *Daily Capital*. On that paper an-other Kansas journalistic luminary—Arthur Capper—started as a 19-year-old typesetter and later became its publisher. Capper ultimately served as governor of Kansas and as U.S. Senator from that state.

homesteading. Boomerism became a continuing editorial endeavor. Even the devastating grass-hopper plague of 1874 and equally disastrous drouth years failed to dim the ardor of Kansas editors for their state.

The coming of the railroads introduced still another factor to the Kansas economy. It was discovered that cattle not only would grow fat during the summer on the hardy grass of the plains, but they prospered during the winter on the nutritious dried forage. After 1866 millions of acres of range lands were opened, and Kansas became the terminus of such famed cattle byways as the Chisholm Trail. Abilene, Wichita, Hays, Great Bend and Dodge City were among the num-erous cow-towns which sprang up along the rail lines. The newspapers of those hell-for-leather settlements recorded an interesting saga of America's frontier history, replete with such leading characters as Bat Masterson and Wild Bill Hickok.

Unlike most other western states, Kansas could boast that at least two of her editors rose to as much prominence as her gun-slingers. One, of course, was William Allen White (see opposite page), but almost equally as renowned was the "Sage of Potato Hill"—Edgar Watson Howe, publisher of the Atchison *Globe*. White himself said that "E. W. Howe is the most remarkable man Kansas or the Middle West has produced,"

Globe. Almost immediately Ed Howe began to attract attention as a "paragrapher." His pithy comments were copied by editors throughout the land; the *Boston Globe,* for instance, carried 58 Howe-isms in a single issue. What was so unusual was that Howe achieved his fame in God-fearing Kansas while carrying on his unrelenting war against religion and the "weaker sex." People simply *had* to read what he wrote whether it offended them or not!

Other Kansas editors didn't come off quite so well. Col. Dan R. Anthony, the vitriolic publisher of several papers, wrote what he thought,

Kansas publishers made the switch from hand-presses to steam model as soon as they could afford them. *The Daily Champion* of Atchison (above left) proudly announced its "modern" equipment on the front of its building. (Below) The *Kinsley Graphic's* new steam cylinder. (Above) Two ornate Kansas nameplates.

and yet Howe's son called his father "the most wretchedly unhappy man I ever knew."

Howe was born in 1854, sharing his birth-year with the Kansas-Nebraska Act. Son of a Methodist circuit-riding preacher, young Howe was whipped if he fell asleep during six-hour sermons. When he was 14, his Bible-quoting father ran off with a lady member of his congregation. It was little wonder that the teen-age printer's devil developed a permanent hatred of both religion and women.

After a sojourn through the West as a tramp printer, Ed Howe settled down in Atchison where, with $200 and the help of his brother, he began publishing a tiny free daily called *The Little*

(Both papers) The Kansas State Historical Society

THE B-B-BLIZZARD.

Price 10 cents.   KINSLEY, KANSAS, SATURDAY, JAN., 23, 1886.   Vol. 1 No. 1.

LATEST.

Terrors of the Prairies!!!

Locked in the Embrace of the Grim Frost King.

Terrible Sufferings of the Snow-Bound Raymond Excursion Party. Hope Not Yet Wholly Abandoned.

The thousand loving and anxious parents, brothers and sisters, lovers and creditors of the Raymond Excursion party, which left the genial clime and balmy airs of Boston, Orr's Island and Yantic so full of joyous anticipations

doned save for one cheering thought. It is learned that the Meegs elaborate railroad project is being vigorously pushed through, and the horizon is now being anxiously scanned for the first signs of its approach Kinsleyward. Meanwhile cold milk has gone up to $5 a fluid drachm, and unless the Meegs track shall have been pushed to this point by December 31st, 1888, the party must resign themselves to their inevitable fate.   W. H. BACKUS.

COMMUNICATED,

Kinsley, Kansas, Jan. 22, 1886.
DEAR BLIZZARD:—An inhabitant of the metropolis of the northwest is not expected to be unhappy anywhere but least of all when deterred by inclement snows in the heart of Kansas on board a Pullman

tient and entertaining as though he'd never known a pain.
Dr. C. L. Richardson, long officially connected with the celebrated Amoskeag Mills, of Manchester, N. H. is the friend of everybody since he supplied them with calico at 10 cents per yard.
Yours Truly,
NORTHWEST.

SNOWBOUND IN KANSAS.

Two A.T. & S. F. R. R. Passenger Trains Motionless at This Point. Three Hundred Discontented Passengers.

The through west-bound passenger train arrived here January 26th, 12:25 a. m., and could proceed no further on account of the heavy snow drifts which

peculiarity of the statutes or constitution of Colorado. To say the least of it, we are in hopes that the law of this state does not justify such a decision.

PRATT COUNTY is a field of battle. The war over the county seat question there came very near culminating in a bloody contest a short time since. The contesting towns being Pratt Center and Saratoga. The county seat has heretofore been located at Saratoga. At the election last November the proposition of removing the county seat to Pratt Center was voted upon. The county commissioners favored the removal, and as there was more votes cast in Saratoga precinct than there were men, women and children living in it, they refused to canvass the vote of that precinct and declared the result in

(Above) The heavy snows of 1886 created a unique, short-lived newspaper called *The B-B-Blizzard*. It was printed in Kingsley where two trains of the Atchison, Topeka & Santa Fe were marooned with some 300 passengers. (Right) Manuscript newspapers were not uncommon in frontier journalism, and Barton County, Kansas, boasted *The Red-wing Carrier Pigeon* in the 1880s.

too, but as a result he was—at one time or another—horse-whipped, beaten with an umbrella, punched in the nose and seriously wounded by gunfire. Still another editor, J. Clarke Swayze of the *Topeka Daily Blade,* was shot to death by John W. Wilson of the *Topeka Commonwealth* in 1877 after Swayze accused Wilson and his father of padding their bills for public printing.

Obviously there was excitement in Kansas journalism—and there was variety, too. The indomitable Carrie Nation published her *Smasher's Mail* to promote the cause of temperance (see page 174). In his *Lucifer The Light-Bearer,* published at Valley Falls, Editor Moses Harman advocated free love. Rev. Charles M. Sheldon edited *The Topeka Daily Capital* for an entire week "as Jesus would have done it." The *Appeal to Reason,* emanating from Girard, Kansas, was for two decades one of the strongest voices for Socialism and organized labor in America. In 1873 the *Smith County Pioneer* printed for the first time the words of the famous ballad, "Home on the Range," written by Dr. Brewster Higley. Discovery of the paper ended a long controversy over the song's authorship.

No wonder Kansas has won a unique spot in the story of American journalism! Her editors have run the gamut of ideas; several have at-

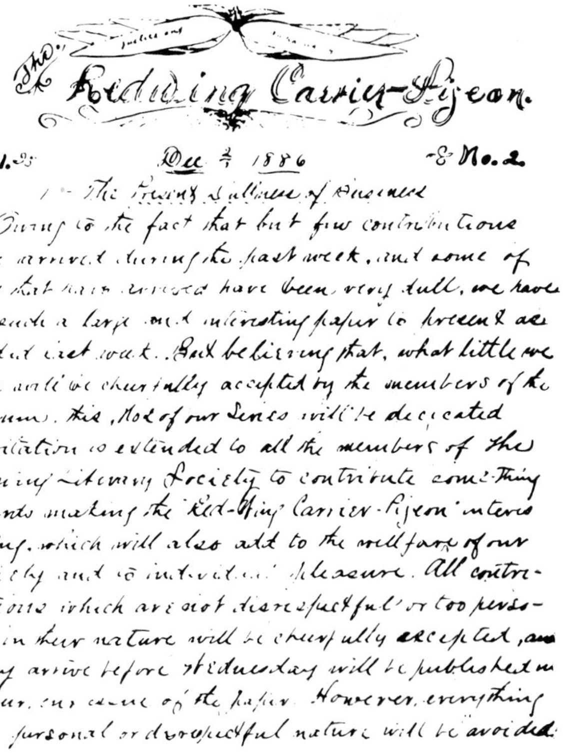

The Redwing Carrier-Pigeon.

Vol. 1.   Dec 4 1886   No. 2

[handwritten manuscript newspaper content, largely illegible]

tained lasting fame; few states have had as many gazettes to chronicle their early histories. Somewhat like Nebraska, Kansas was a through-way to frontiers farther west, and itinerant printers came and went across her broad expanse. In the early 1830's Jotham Meeker noted that he paid $468.13 in Cincinnati to outfit the entire shop of the *Shawnee Sun*. From that modest beginning a vital industry grew and prospered. But in final analysis, men, not equipment, made newspapering in early-day Kansas the warm, personal, vibrant calling it was. They were men like Sol Miller of Troy, who, in the dramatic pre-Civil War era, recognized one prime mission: "To get the *Chief*

(Above) Old-time printers of the *Dodge City Globe-Republican*. (Below) Few early newspapers had as ornate a front office advertising-and-subscription counter as the *Hutchinson News*. (Below left) As early as 1875 Russian immigrants in southeast Kansas voiced their philosophies through *The Progressive Communist*.

THE PROGRESSIVE COMMUNIST

JUSTICE AND FRATERNITY

VOL. I.   PROGRESSIVE COMMUNITY KANSAS, JULY 1875.   No. 7.

INSPIRATIONAL POEM.

E. M. PEARSALL, MEDIUM.

Come Holy Spirit from above,
With thy blessed influence sweet,
Oh, fill our souls with heavenly love
As we together meet.

Ye loving angels pure and bright,
Sweet inspiration give;
Come from your home of peace and light
And teach us how to live.

Oh! help us guide the weary soul
Whose life is sad and lone,
To point him to the joys above
In yon bright spirit home.

Oh! give us strength to labor here
Our mission to fulfil.
Oh! banish all distrust and fear,
And guide and keep us still.

The Division.

By the way our correspondence has fallen off, and by the the tone of some of the letters which we have received we should think that the impression has gone abroad that the PROGRESSIVE COMMUNITY is about breaking up. Nothing is further from the fact. We are more united and determined than ever before. There has been nothing but a formal division into what we have been socially all the time: two communities.

There are now, of us, three men, three women, one boy fifteen, and three smaller children; and others have promised to join us as soon as we are ready to receive them; The division causes some temporary inconvenience, but will be no permanent injury to the Community, and the future looks as bright as ever. We have now made arrangements by which

Some of the farmers about us are threshing their wheat, and we hear of enormous yields. Three different fields turned out forty bushels, and over, to the acre, and the *Howard County Ledger* tells of one acre that produced 75 bus. This together with the facts that wheat has never failed since this country was settled and that the best winter wheat is raised, indicates that this is one of the best, if not the very best wheat country east of the Rocky Mountains if not in America. Our wheat was light on account of being sown late, and being pastured some in the winter; it was winter killed. The grasshoppers scare prevented us from putting it in earlier.

It may seem strange that the complaint about too much wet should come from "Drouthy Kansas," yet we are now obliged to make it. It rains so frequently

out on time." They were men like William Allen White, who reminisced about his work on the *Emporia Daily News:* "I pounded the streets in the afternoons for items, went to the railroad station, rode the fire wagon, chased the runaway horses of the grocer's delivery wagon, and made myself generally useful in the literature of the time and the place—prouder than Pontius Pilate of my reporting job in the big-town newspaper office."

They were men like Editor Louden who made it a weekly practice on publishing day to walk around the square in Delphos and announce proudly to all businessmen: "The *Herald's* out!" Then on June 10, 1879, a tornado smashed the town, wrecked the printing plant and injured the editor. But Louden didn't give up easily. Picking his type out of the littered street, he painfully produced his next edition. Kansas journalism was like that!

Some of the old photos of early-day journalism were stiff, posed and cliche-ridden. Doubtless, the reporters of the *Hutchinson News (above)* didn't dress like that every day, nor did the young lady always wear her Sunday bonnet when she took dictation from the editor. Back-shop pictures were often similarly hammed-up, although the printers of the *Russell Record (below)* didn't appear to be more than momentarily disrupted from their task of hand-spiking another edition. Such photos, however, help portray the atmosphere of pre-1900 journalism better than most diaries or memoirs.

Montana - Idaho:

Printing Presses in Eldorado

"Blessed Be the Man Who Payeth the Printer."

Lewiston Teller
April 10, 1890

THE METALLIC WEALTH ON BOTH sides of the Continental Divide became a giant magnet which lured gold-seekers to the rugged back-country of Idaho and Montana. Fur trappers and traders, zealous missionaries, adventuresome trail-blazers and a few aimless wanderers had preceded the hopeful miners to Grasshopper Creek, Last Chance Gulch and the Coeur d'Alene country. Until gold was discovered, however, there was little need for newspapers. The first development came in what is now Idaho when rich strikes were made on the Salmon and Clearwater Rivers in 1860. The tent city of Lewiston was the closest supply point to the new bonanza, so it was the logical spot for A. S.

(Opposite page) This picturesque structure was the first newspaper office in Billings, M.T. (Above) *The Montana Post* was printed in the rear of the City Book Store in Virginia City. (Right) Idaho's first newspaper was *The Golden Age,* founded by A. S. Gould in Lewiston (then in Washington Territory) on August 2, 1862.

(Opposite page) Historical Society of Montana

THE GOLDEN AGE.

University of Idaho Library

Idaho Historical Society

Gould to establish *The Golden Age,* the state's first newspaper.

As if the physical problems of starting a newspaper in the back country weren't bad enough, Gould's *Golden Age* was a Republican sheet in a town settled by miners and Confederates. The courageous editor (about whom little else is known, incidentally) unfurled Lewiston's first U.S. flag over his print shop. Retaliation was quick. Twenty-one shots were fired into it by "dis-union Democrats."

The Golden Age first appeared on August 2, 1862, and Gould added to his problems by denouncing the miners for their treatment of the Indians. The record shows that while the paper lasted through Lewiston's brief period as the Idaho territorial capital, the editor disappeared after the first issue.

(Above) This dilapidated building housed the historic Spalding Mission at Lapwai, scene of the first printing in the Pacific Northwest. Missionary-printer E. O. Hall published religious materials for the Nez Perce Indians. (Left) Alonzo Leland was one of Idaho's most versatile newspapermen. An attorney, surveyor and political leader, he edited *The Golden Age* in 1864. In 1876 he and his son, Charles, founded *The Lewiston Teller,* which promoted the annexation of Northern Idaho to Washington Territory.

The **Idaho Tri-Weekly Statesman** was not originally intended to be a Boise newspaper. James S. Reynolds, a young journalist from Maine, fully intended to establish a paper in Idaho City with the help of two printers, Tom and Dick Reynolds (no relation). Enroute to Idaho City, with their equipment in an ox-drawn wagon, the printers were intercepted by H. C. Riggs, who had been delegated by the citizens of Boise to find an editor willing to start a paper in Boise. He offered a stipend of $1,500, plus the use of an office building free for a year.

The proposal sounded so good that Tom Reynolds jumped on a horse and galloped to Idaho City to tell James, who had ridden ahead to make preparations for the newspaper in that settlement. The proposition made sense to him, too, so the freight wagon was turned around and pointed toward Boise. The "office" turned out to be a crude hut with dirt floor, glassless windows and an entrance without a door. In spite of these shortcomings, the Reynolds trio went to work in the heat of the summer sun, and on July 26, 1864, the first copy of the **Idaho Tri-Weekly Statesman** came off the Washington hand-press.

Like most frontier papers, the **Statesman** had its troubles. Editor Reynolds carried no firearms, but he wisely kept an iron bar, a wagon spoke, an ax handle and a couple of old horse pistols within easy reach for self-protection. In the 1870s hungry Indians somehow discovered that one of the main ingredients in press rollers was molasses—so, according to at least one historian, they stole the rollers which they ate like candy.

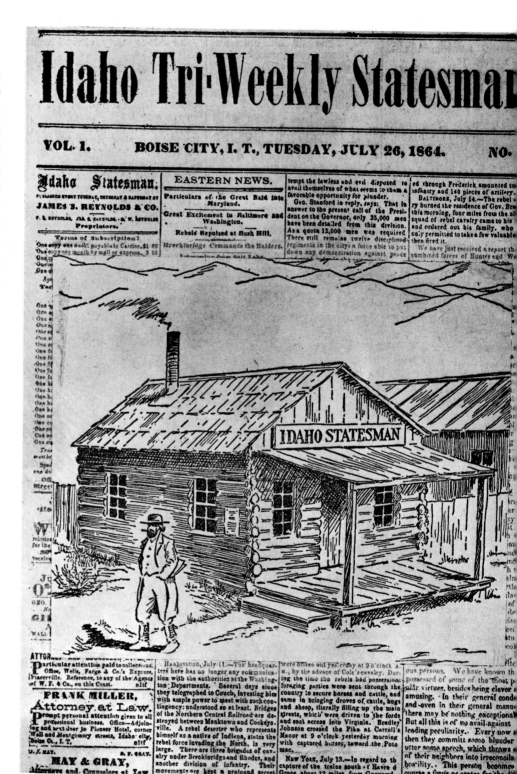

Idaho Statesman Sketch

Interestingly enough, another press had operated in that same area more than two decades earlier. East of Lewiston, at the Lapwai Indian Mission, Edwin O. Hall had printed an eight-page booklet in the Nez Perce language in May of 1839. While neither Hall nor other missionary-printers who succeeded him produced anything resembling a newspaper, they brought to Idaho the honor of the first printing in the Pacific Northwest.

The early settlement of Idaho was somewhat unique because it was accomplished by an eastward movement. When gold was discovered, no-

(Above) Compared to its early predecessors, the *Boise Citizen* was published in sheer luxury, with a floor, windows and a powered press. (Below) The *Idaho World* was a partisan Democratic paper which succeeded the *Boise News* at Idaho City in 1865.

madic miners from Oregon and California rushed to the new diggings. The famed Mullan Road from Walla Walla through the rugged wilderness to Fort Benton became a busy thoroughfare for optimistic prospectors.

Meanwhile, however, the first newspapers were concentrated at Lewiston, Idaho City and Boise. The shift of the territorial capital to the latter settlement created a fiery issue in Lewiston and for the newspapers which followed *The Golden Age.* The *North Idaho Radiator* and *The Lewiston Teller* led unsuccessful campaigns to have Northern Idaho annexed to Washington Territory. Other controversial subjects of the day included the slavery question, the mass influx of Chinese laborers and the ever-present Indian problems.

More productive gold discoveries in the Boise Basin lured the population southward. At Bannock (later Idaho City) Tom and John Butler got out *The Boise News,* using a tobacco box tin

for a composing stick, a planed log for a stone and a chase made from old horseshoe iron. Having the only press in the area, the brothers made the most of it by issuing campaign papers for both political parties.

The 1860s were boom years in southern Idaho. At least 14 newspapers prospered during the decade, only four of which survived when the placer mining era declined. The later gold discoveries in the Coeur d'Alenes brought a new burst of interest and, as usual, printers were in the vanguard. Typical of the breed was 39-year-old Adam Aulbach who hauled a complete printing outfit into the mountains strapped on the backs of 45 mules. At Murray he started setting type in a log cabin on July 2, 1884, intending to publish his *Idaho Sun* on the Fourth of July. While he was working, his competitor—Henry Bernard of the *Coeur d'Alene Pioneer*—shot and killed a typesetter in the *Pioneer* plant, and Aulbach delayed his publication until July 8 to get all the facts.

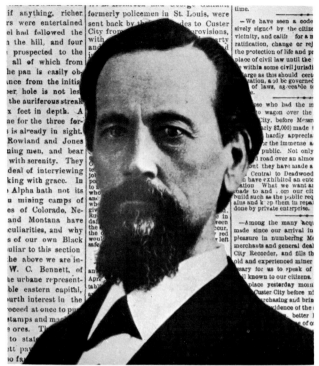

(Below) This much-traveled Washington hand-press made the long trip around Cape Horn to Portland, Oregon. After service there and later in Walla Walla, it was hauled by wagon to Idaho City where it produced the *News* and its successor, the *Idaho World*. (Above right) Thomas J. Butler and his brother brought journalism to Boise in 1863. (Right) Promotion of a wagon train to the Idaho gold fields.

PUBLIC NOTICE!!

BEST ROUTE TO
GOLD MINES
OF
IDAHO!

The undersigned, having been appointed under Act of Congress, Superintendent for the establishing of the Wagon and Emigrant Road to Idaho, via, the Niobrara Valley, hereby gives notice, That a Train of Freight and Emigrant Wagons, with the Construction Teams and hands, and a Government Escort of 200 Cavalry, and Battery of Artillery will leave Sioux City, Iowa about, the middle of May next for Gallatin and Virginia cities and Idaho and Montana Territories. The route will be up the Valley of the Niobrara thence direct to Gallatin City, crossing Tongue River where Gen. Sully's fort for the protection of the Emigrants in the

BLACK HILLS OF DAKOTA

Is to be established, and reaching Gallatin City about 700 miles travel from the mouth of the Niobrara, and passing over a fertile, well watered and wooded country, and is altogether the best, and several hundred miles the shortest route to the Gold Mines of Idaho. The Escort will afford ample protection, and it is expected that the Train will move along with little or no delay.

All persons wishing to go by this route, are desired to be on hand by the time of starting.
JAMES A. SAWYERS, Superintendent.

Sioux City, Iowa, April 12, 1865.
Northwestern Papers, please Notice.

THE NEWS LETTER.

VOL. I. HELENA, M. T., SATURDAY, JULY 24, 1875. NO. 7.

THE NEWS LETTER

PUBLISHED EVERY SATURDAY BY

ALLEN & TRAVIS.

TERMS OF SUBSCRIPTION:

One Year, - - - - $2 00
Single Copy, - - - 5
Per Month, Delivered by Carrier, - 25

TO THE PUBLIC.

It was our intention to have issued the first number of the DAILY NEWS-LETTER on last Tuesday, but circumstances over which we have had no control interfered. The delay is vexatious to us, and the loss has been considerable, but on next Tuesday we promise the daily, and ask for it the kind consideration of the public. That it will be a success we cannot doubt; for with hardly an exception, the public commend the enterprise, and bid God-speed.

In this connection we desire to again call your attention to our facilities for executing plain and ornamental printing. We have secured the services of a competent job printer whose experience in the art of printing is to us ample assurance that the class of work

and cliques have accomplished: swallowed up, as it were, stock, bonds and all, and left the credulous public in the lurch; there is no need to refer to the evils wrought by subsidies, we have an example close to our borders. If we want a railroad, and we do, let us build it ourselves.

Any careful observer of the development of railroads from their inception to the present day, will not fail to notice that private enterprise has achieved by far the most beneficial results. Where the people individually and collectively, build, own and control a railroad, the evils referred to cannot invade a corporation of such strength. But this is not the only reason why a railroad should be ours in inception and completion; this is of course only a question of time, so was the completion of the N. P. R. R., and is likely to be for the next decade, we want it on short notice and the sooner the better. Let a monopoly or ring get hold of it and we run the same desperate chances; let it be subsidized and we will not be better off, unless it be subsidized to a limitless extent, of which there is no possibility; but let us take hold of the matter ourselves, issue stock, solicit

opened and worked, and social and commercial relations will receive an impetus which will place us on an equal footing with our more favored sister territories and states.

E. M. HOYT,

REAL ESTATE and mining agent, Main street Helena.

Will buy, sell, hire, collect rents, and transact all business in this department for residents and non-residents.

Will buy, sell, or otherwise negotiate any and all transactions in both quartz and placer interests at home and abroad,

M. REINIG,

VEGETABLE DEPOT, Bridge street. Groceries, wines, liquors and produce. Montana vegetables always on hand in their season. Particular attention paid to supplying gulches.

NEW GOODS JUST RECEIVED!

AT J. T. WARD'S, consisting of a well-selected stock of stationery, latest styles of legal fold papers, and everything connected with the trade, which he offers at bed-rock rates. Call and examine for yourself.

FRED LEHMAN,

DEALER IN GROCERIES, liquors, cigars, tobacco, grain, and farmers' produce. All goods first-class. Free delivery in the city. No. 3 Main St. Helena.

DAVIS & WALLACE,

RETAIL DEALERS in choice family

(Left) There were a number of teen-age editors in Old West journalism. One of them was Lee Travis, a 14-year-old Helena publisher whose *News Letter* was not a play-thing but a full-fledged newspaper. In addition to handling all the editorial and printing chores, young Travis traveled over three rugged counties in a buckboard promoting subscriptions for his paper. Before he died of acute bronchitis in 1882 at the age of 21, Travis was a respected newsman who had established several territorial newspapers, among them the Helena *Morning Capital.* (Below) A post-gold rush paper in Virginia City was *The Madisonian* founded in 1873. Its columns chronicled the continuing story of Alder Gulch after *The Montana Post* had been moved to Helena. This photo was taken in *The Madisonian's* editorial office before the turn of the century.

Historical Society of Montana

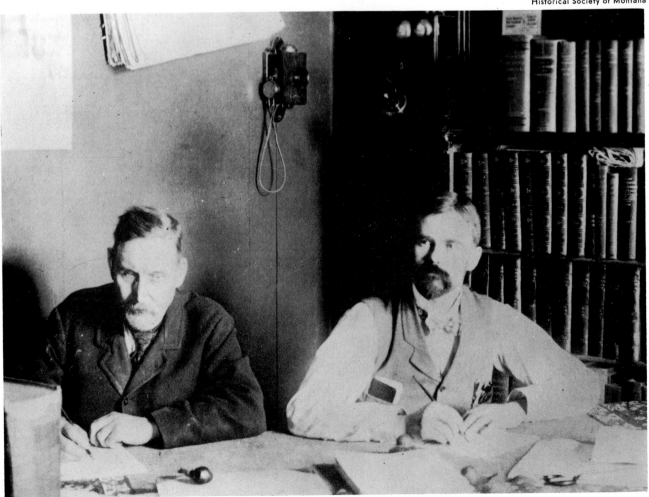

96

Professor Thomas Josiah Dimsdale came to Virginia City in 1863, not for gold but for his health. The cultured young Englishman was frail and tubercular. Unable to work in the mines, he conducted a private school, charging $2 a week for each pupil. When Montana became a territory, Gov. Sidney Edgerton named Dimsdale superintendent of education. With few official duties involved because of the lack of schools, he had plenty of time to devote to the editorship of **The Montana Post**, which he brightened with his wit and acid pen.

Dimsdale's greatest fame came, however, through a series of articles about the lawlessness on the Bannack-Virginia City road. His "Vigilantes of Montana," the state's first book, was a collection of these articles. It has since become a classic in Western Americana.

Though he was extremely sensitive and physically weak, the unlikely frontier editor with the Oxford accent bucked his predominantly Confederate readers and entertained at political rallies with his sardonic humor. He coughed away his life on September 26, 1866, at the age of 35.

THE MONTANA POST.

B. W. TILTON, & CO., Editors & Proprietors.   "My Country, May she Always be right, But My Country, Right or Wrong."   TERMS:—$7.50 In Gold For Year in Adva

VOL. I.   CITY OF VIRGINIA, MONTANA TERRITORY, SATURDAY, APRIL 29, 1865.   NO.

Montana State Press Association

But if Idaho journalism was rough-and-tumble, newspapering in Montana was even more so. Again it was gold which opened the territory and set the stage for excitement, drama and violence. The first rich strikes were made on Grasshopper Creek in July of 1862, and almost overnight the town of Bannack sprang up. Miners came over the mountains from the west and northward from Colorado, anxious to try their luck in still another Eldorado.

The inevitable occurred, of course, and printing presses were on the scene almost as soon as the first gold pans. There has long been conjecture about what was Montana's first journal, but of the three publications started in 1864, only one— *The Montana Post*—appears to have the qualifications of a true newspaper. In Bannack (the temporary territorial capital), Francis M. Thompson is known to have published a small sheet known as the *East Bannack News Letter*. A few

In 1866 four brothers—James, Robert, Daniel and Andrew Fisk—came to Montana. Robert, the eldest, was a printer who acquired the worn-out type and press of the old *Radiator*, and on November 15, 1886, the first issue of the *Helena Weekly Herald* was produced. The paper ultimately became the first daily in the state. This photo of the *Herald* building was taken in the mid-1880s when the paper was actively promoting statehood for the territory.

Historical Society of Montana

weeks earlier, several young men issued a tiny paper in Virginia City. John A. Creighton, benefactor of Creighton University in Omaha, acted as the printer's devil for the venture—and reputedly provided six bottles of champagne for the crew. Possibly that is why nobody to this day remembers the name of that paper!

The unbelievably rich placer deposits in Alder Gulch created Virginia City—and there, in a log building with sod roof, John Buchanan and Marion M. Manners printed *The Montana Post* for the first time on August 27, 1864. The struggle of bringing a heavy printing press up the Missouri by steamboat to Fort Benton and then overland to the gold country was worth it as they sold out their first issue of 960 copies at 50 cents each. After a couple of issues, Buchanan sold the entire operation for $3,000 to Daniel W. Tilton and Benjamin R. Dittes, who printed it in the

Courtesy of Daniel B. Hertz, Jr.

(Left) One of the pioneer papers of Deer Lodge, Mont., was the *Silver State*. Printer Daniel B. Hertz, Jr., with suspenders, later served as a county official for half a century. **(Below)** Frank B. Linderman, in the printer's apron, bought *The Chinook* in Sheridan, Mont., for a $5 down payment. To make the enterprise pay, he also operated a furniture store and assay office.

Historical Society of Montana

back of Tilton's book store. When Helena started to surpass Virginia City, *The Post* was moved there, only to become the victim of the disastrous fire of 1869 and a stack of unpaid bills.

The Montana Post played an important role in one of the territory's most violent chapters. The rich placer deposits at Alder Gulch had created the new mining camp some 90 miles east of Bannack. The Confederate miners tried to name the settlement Varina in honor of Mrs. Jefferson Davis, but it became Virginia City instead. Soon there were thousands of boisterous gold-seekers in the Gulch, and the road between the new settlement and Bannack was alive with stagecoaches, freight wagons and individual riders. With so much gold being hauled back and forth between the two camps, the setup was ideal for road agents—and the ensuing era of lawlessness was unique in the annals of the West.

Arch villain of the drama was Henry Plummer —a murderer, gambler and woman-chaser still in his twenties—who somehow managed to become sheriff of the district encompassing the two

This vintage photo was taken in Helena after *The Montana Post* was shifted there from Virginia City (top). Before the move its earlier home was given a new face. (Left) Like most frontier newspapers, *The Post* depended upon its job department to provide operating revenue.

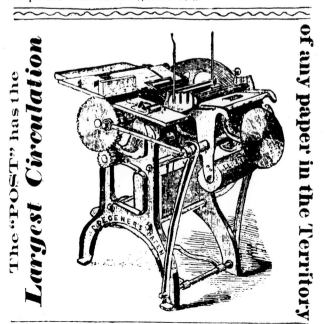

THE
Montana Post

Job Printing of all Kinds—Cards, Billheads, Ball Tickets, Show Cards, Wedding and Visiting Cards, Posters, Hand-Bills, Circulars, Theater Programmes, etc.,—done at the POST JOB OFFICE in the best style and at low prices. Satisfaction guaranteed.

The "POST" has the *Largest Circulation* of any paper in the Territory

camps. What followed was a year of calloused slaughter and plundering along the 90-mile road with the sheriff as the leader of the desperadoes. By the end of 1863 more than 100 travelers had been murdered and uncounted hoards of gold stolen.

The ultimate result was the formation of a secret society of Vigilantes, pledged to seek out and destroy the villains. These determined citizens defied Sheriff Plummer and his organized criminals and proceeded to take the law into their own hands. Between December 20, 1863, and

Historical Society of Montana

by 15-year-old J. Allen Hosmer, one of two teen-age editors in the state's frontier era. Even while Virginia City was in its hey-day, a new rival began to emerge. Last Chance Gulch proved a fabulously wealthy strike, and Helena—with the accent on "hell"—was founded. Its first news-paper was *The Montana Radiator,* printed on the press of the earlier *Radiator* at Lewiston. The same press produced the state's first daily, the *Helena Herald.* By 1875, when Helena succeeded Virginia City as the territorial capital, it was already the region's most important news center.

Typical of other western states, Montana and Idaho found stability after the gold-boom period. Mining remained a most important industry, but agriculture, lumbering and the advent of the railroads helped establish permanent towns rather than capricious gold camps. As early as 1866 the first great cattle drive from Texas was conducted by Nelson Story of Bozeman. The romantic era of the cowboy was born, reaching its peak when the railroads made possible a string of "cow towns" like Billings, Miles City, Culbertson and Havre. Each soon had at least one newspaper.

Late in the century Montana experienced the famous Battle of the Copper Kings as William A. Clark, Marcus Daly and F. Augustus Heinze vied for control. Newspapers became tools of their struggle which was concentrated in the Butte area. Talented reporters and editorial writers were imported to manage the news and to

February 5, 1864, they tried and hanged 24 felons, including the miscreant sheriff.

This period of lawlessness preceded journalism in the area, but the report of "The Vigilantes of Montana" which appeared in *The Montana Post* beginning in August of 1865 became a classic in Western literature. Prof. Thomas J. Dimsdale— the cultured, tubercular editor of the paper— wrote a series of articles about the bloody epoch. These articles were later reprinted in Montana's first book.

While the Virginia City-Bannack episode was extreme in nature, other gold camps did not lack for violence of their own. Animosities stirred by the Civil War, hatred of the Chinese, the con-tinuing Indian raids and the political growing pains of a rough-hewn region provided editors with reams of zestful copy.

Virginia City took the lead in early Montana journalism, with *The Post* soon followed by the *Montana Democrat* and an interesting sheet called *The Beaver Head News.* The latter was published

(Left above) *The Eagle's Nest* at Ekalaka, Mont., featured a flamboyant office front. Note the editor's head on the eagle. (Below) In the 1870s ornate nameplates became more and more common on frontier newspapers.

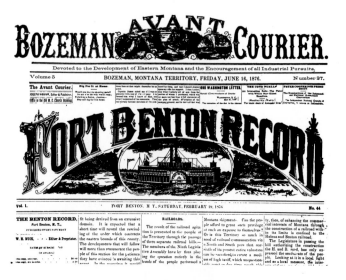

100

mold public opinion. Meanwhile, the press of both Idaho and Montana became involved in the fight for Free Silver, and in the process the *Idaho World* even went so far as to describe President Cleveland as a "thick-skulled, big-necked, beefy Mogul . . ."

All was not gloom, brimstone, malice and greed, however; there was always a lighter side. The same *Idaho World* was proud of its office cat named Belshazzar which won a big bet for its printer-owners by climbing a greased pole. Numerous editors regaled the ladies for using rolled-up newspapers for bustles. In a parade to celebrate statehood, the *North Idaho Star* of Moscow had its operations temporarily disrupted when a press fell off a float and was demolished. Printers squandered their paychecks over the weekend, tippling with the best of them and "jeffing quads," the latter being a gambling game in which type quads were thrown like dice.

In a way newspapering itself was a gamble, and those who played the game on the frontier won or lost on the turn of a press wheel. It was exciting and promising—but the odds were great!

Historical Society of Montana

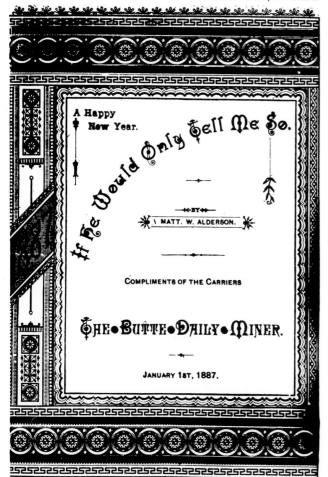

Historical Society of Montana

Montana State Press Association

(Top) *The Tribune* office in Lewiston, Idaho, circa 1898. (Left) Throughout the West it was a New Year's custom for newsboys to deliver a "carrier's address"—after which the boys received a tip or a treat. *The Butte Daily Miner* published this "address" in 1887. (Bottom) Capt. James Hamilton Mills was known as a "king among territorial editors." He founded the *New Northwest* in Deer Lodge in 1869.

101

Nebraska:

The Printer Tramps Westward

"You cannot have a good town without a good news-paper, and with a genuine up-to-date paper a town cannot long remain obscure and uninteresting."

George T. Hammond
Nebraska Editor, 1896

Nebraska, land of "shallow waters," played a unique but vitally important role in the development of the West.

As a matter of fact, it wasn't Nebraska as much as it was the Platte and the Niobrara Rivers which offered the natural by-ways to the promised land beyond. Across the vast undulating prairies, broken only by isolated buttes and occasional ragged little canyons, rolled the wagon trains and ox carts of emigrants seeking homes in Oregon, gold in California and religious haven in Utah. Also tramping to new frontiers were eager editors and printers!

At first, few of those traveling westward with stars in their eyes found incentive enough to settle in Nebraska. It was merely the highway to

(Opposite page) The sod house was the symbol of frontier Nebraska. Appropriately, at least one newspaper—the *Broken Bow Republican*—was produced in a "soddy." (Above) Moving day for the Kearney *New Era* typified that most early papers were relatively mobile, having only the bare essentials in equipment and supplies. (Below) Mergers, name-changes and hyphenated titles were common. The *New Era* above ultimately became the *New Era-Standard*.

Western History Research Center, University of Wyoming

With the railroad, newspapering came to Nebraska in earnest. Presses appeared along the right-of-way to bring the news to sparsely populated junctions and spirited "cow towns" like Ogallala, Sidney and Schuyler. In fact, newspapers were actually printed on the trains themselves as this sketch from *Frank Leslie's Illustrated* shows. Impressions were pulled on an "Army Press," so-called because it was a model used by military units on the frontier.

Ultimately, hundreds of newspapers throughout the West owed their existence to these portable proof presses which adventuresome young printers and editors hand-carried to lumber camps and mining towns. (Below) When the Pullman Hotel Express connected East with West, the *Trans-Continental* was published daily aboard the train, probably in much the same manner as *Leslie's* artist depicted above.

Eldorado and the bountiful lushness of the Pacific Northwest.

But gradually a change took place. Along the western trail, the trading posts and military forts gave way to towns. In 1860 the Pony Express

focused further attention on the route to California, and on July 1, 1862, President Lincoln signed "an act to aid in the construction of a Railway and Telegraph line from the Missouri River to the Pacific Ocean." The fact that the line would

"LET EVERY STEP BE AN ADVANCE."

Vol. 1.   Omaha, Neb., May 20, 1870.   No. 2.

follow the 100th meridian assured Nebraska of its own development. The announcement also had a great effect on the development of newspapers along the way.

While the Civil War delayed the building of the railroad, the Free Homestead Act of 1862 brought some settlers hardy enough to tackle the raw prairies. Five years later the Union Pacific Railroad opened a new era for Nebraska, the "Blackwater State," which came into the Union on March 1, 1867, over the veto of President Johnson.

Newspapering, of course, followed this historical development. The first papers appeared along the Missouri River, at the "jumping off"

(Above) Posing with his family before their "soddy," this homesteader was proud to be a subscriber to the *Alliance Independent*. Editors called sod blocks "Nebraska marble." (Right) Railroads promoted homesites by posters and hand-bills. They used this one to entice French families from Canada. (Left) Nebraska newsman Henry Brainerd used this old "Alligator" platen press designed by George Phineas Gordon.

LE CHEMIN DE FER

UNION PACIFIC

A TRAVERS LE

KANSAS ET NEBRASKA

H. W. WEBER,
TOWN TICKET AGENT G. T. R.
24 PITT STREET CORNWALL ONT,

ET

H. W. WEBER,
TOWN TICKET AGENT G. T. R.
24 PITT STREET CORNWALL ONT,

La Celebre Ligne Courte

POUR SE RENDRE EN

Californie   Colorado

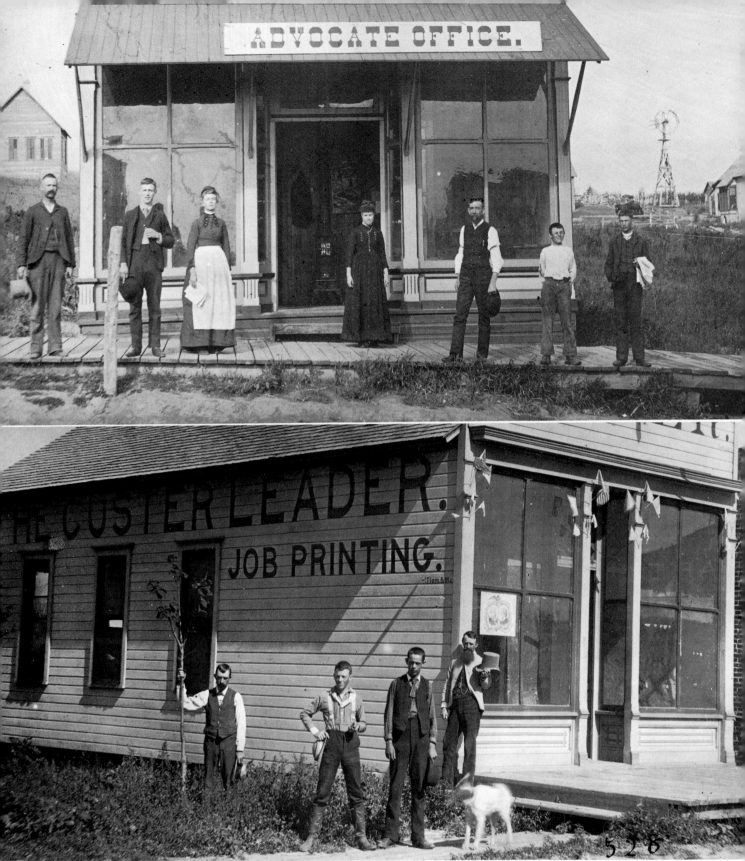

Early-day newspaper buildings had much in common. After he passed the tent, sod-house or log cabin stage, the publisher invariably moved his plant into a "modern" wooden structure, with a squared store front and the inevitable wooden sidewalk. Here are two typical Nebraska newspaper offices, circa 1890: (top) the Ansley *Advocate* and *The Custer County Leader* of Broken Bow. Staffers posed proudly with beavers and **type-sticks**.

places for the westward migration. Oddly enough, the first five Nebraska newspapers were all printed in Iowa.

At St. Mary's, a tiny hamlet just below Bellevue on the Iowa side of the Missouri, *The Nebraska Palladium* was issued by Daniel Reed & Company on July 15, 1854. Not until four months later was it actually printed in Bellevue, to give the new territory its first home-printed journal.

Similarly, the second paper—*The Omaha Arrow*—was first printed in Council Bluffs on July 28, 1854. Editor J. W. Pattison indicated the impecunious condition of the paper when he wrote that the editorial chair was the stump of an ancient oak and the writing table was "the top of our badly abused beaver."

Most of these early Nebraska papers were boomer publications, established more often than not by the town companies eager to promote their chosen sites. A press and an editor were considered vital to the success of a land venture. In

(Above) These citizens of Broken Bow posed before the office of the *Custer County Leader* in 1886. The editor stood in the doorway with type-stick poised. No doubt the youngsters in the front row delivered the paper when it came off the hand-powered press each week. (Below) Job printing for the railroads was an important source of revenue for a few fortunate papers. The *Omaha Republican* produced this land poster.

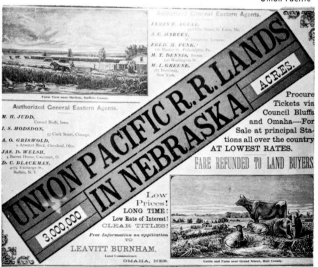

Anyone with tall corn or a tall tale always brought it to the frontier editor. In Dawson County, Nebraska, a favorite gathering place was the office of the *Overton* *Herald*. Subscribers such as these often couldn't afford the price of the paper so they bartered labor, garden products or other edibles with the editor.

1855 the first territorial legislature incorporated 17 towns, and soon little promotion journals were being shipped eastward to attract settlers to the virtually non-existent "cities." J. Sterling Morton, who helped beat the editorial drums for Nebraska City, described the practice thusly: "Young Chicagos, increscent New Yorks, precocious Philadelphias, and infant Londons were duly staked out, lithographed, divided into shares, and puffed with becoming unction and complaisance."

The original *Palladium,* for instance, was really a product of the Bellevue Town Company which had visions of converting a tiny mission and Peter A. Sarpy's trading post into a giant capital

city . . . "the center of commerce, and the half-way house between the Atlantic and the Pacific Oceans." Ultimately more successful, however, was the Council Bluffs and Nebraska Ferry Company which proposed to establish "Omaha City" at a boat landing across the Missouri River from Council Bluffs. On July 4, 1854, the company staged a picnic on the townsite, and a log cabin was partly constructed that day. In less than three weeks, *The Arrow* was singing the praises of the little shack-town as if it were a glamorous metropolis. Unlike many of the boomer papers, *The Arrow* was more prophetic as Omaha prospered while the other townsites failed to live up to their advance promotion.

With the ice broken, printers and newsmen began to move into the territory from neighboring states. The Kansas-Nebraska Act and the slave question did not create the same violent situation which Kansas publishers experienced, but early Nebraska editors made up for that with their own internal political battles. When they weren't boosting their new towns, they were lambasting "copperheadism" or "black Republican rascality," depending, of course, upon their particular inclinations.

By the start of the Civil War there were newspapers not only along the Missouri River, but inland as well. Joseph E. Johnson, a Mormon who had edited *The Arrow* after retracing his steps from Utah, moved westward from Council Bluffs in 1859 to establish the *Huntsman's Echo* on the Wood River near the present town of Shelton. Circulated among emigrants and freighters on the Oregon Trail, the *Echo* attracted many settlers to central Nebraska with its glowing descriptions of the region.

As it happened elsewhere, though, one of the

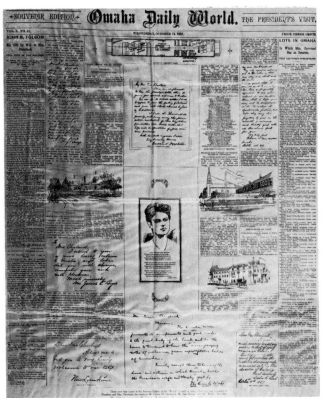

Union Pacific

(Above right) Some frontier publishers printed on cloth because of paper shortages. In 1887, however, the *Omaha Daily World* printed just four copies of its October 12 edition on satin in honor of a visit to that city by President Cleveland. (Below) The *Guide Rock Signal:* a typical small Nebraska newspaper plant.

Mrs. Gertrude Lambert Crary

Washington County (Neb.) Historical Museum (Mrs. Zelma Strode)

While newspapering has always had a ring of glamour to it, the plants of early-day journals were seldom pretentious, seldom neat. Pot-bellied stoves, and later jerry-rigged electrical fixtures, accounted for the numerous fires which wiped out valuable old files. This was the shop of the *Blair* (Neb.) *Tribune.*

greatest boons to newspapering in frontier Nebraska was the Homestead Act of 1862. Not only did it bring the subscribers to read the hand-spiked gazettes, but the legal advertising required under the law released the editors from financial dependence upon land speculation companies. Some publishers profiteered; most, however, had at least some feeling for their journalistic calling and endeavored to produce the best newspaper which conditions and their talents permitted.

It was not easy. The *Broken Bow Republican* was published in a "soddy" (see page 102) 75 miles from the railroad. Its equipment was crude, and its news coverage slim—but its weekly edition was more eagerly awaited than many of today's metropolitan dailies. Revenue was meager and often in kind. On one occasion the publisher accepted a bronco from a subscriber and promptly turned it over to a young typesetter in lieu of a month's wages.

Not far from Broken Bow, *The Merna Record* was started with a bank loan of $120 in a rent-free room behind a photo gallery. When Emerson Purcell, who was not yet of voting age, produced the first copy of *The Record,* snow was blowing in one end of the unfinished room, and the building owner was feeding the pot-bellied stove with ten-cent corn to keep the ink from freezing.

Such journalistic hardships were commonplace. In addition, at least one Nebraska editor was killed for writing unpopular opinions, while the *Nebraska State Journal* was one of the few newspapers ever hanged in effigy. It editorially supported a new trial for a horse thief, and the citizens of Minden didn't like it! For a time (circa 1872) Norfolk had a manuscript paper for which the editor accepted wheat, potatoes, eggs and mink skins, small solace for a bad case of writer's cramp.

After its inauspicious beginning, Omaha became Nebraska's major city and, consequently, its chief news center. Starting with the absentee *Arrow,* it has had numerous journals through the span of years. In 1860 the *Omaha Daily Telegraph* became the territory's first daily. The *Omaha Republican* boasted the area's first power-driven press. One of the most influential papers in the city was the *Omaha Daily Herald,* founded in 1865 and edited by Dr. George L. Miller, Omaha's first physician and a visionary who contributed much to the city's development. In 1871 a Jewish-Bohemian immigrant named Edward Rosewater established the *Omaha Bee* and the Bohemian-language *Pokrok Zapadu (Progress of the West),* one of numerous foreign-language papers printed in the state whose cheap prairie lands had attracted thousands of ambitious aliens.

Several consolidations and mergers resulted in the creation of the *Omaha World-Herald,* once edited by William Jennings Bryan before he started his own paper, *The Commoner,* in Lincoln. The emergence of Bryan as a presidential candidate grew out of great turmoil in Nebraska, all of which is preserved on the yellowed pages of the state's old newspapers. Grasshopper plagues, drouth, starvation prices for crops and prohibitive shipping charges brought about such movements as the Grange, the Farmers Alliance and Populism. Papers were spiced with reports of such political activities, and controversy was rampant. Nebraska publishers fired editorial broadsides with the best of them, and from sod house to beef-baron mansion, their newspapers were avidly read, violently hated or ardently believed. The Prairie Press was potent indeed!

(Above) The *Nebraska Democrat,* a Grand Island newspaper, was a promoter of Free Silver and the Populist movement which swept across the state in the last two decades of the 19th century. (Below) William H. Mullane published *The Keith County News* in this tiny building in Ogallala, Nebraska's "Cowboy Capital." *The News* was later published by Anna Gray Clark, a teacher.

Courtesy of C. J. Triplett, Jr.

𝔑evada:

Chroniclers of the Comstock

*"That of twenty men, nineteen patronize the saloon
and one the newspaper, and I am going for the
crowd."*

W. J. Forbes
The Daily Trespass
Virginia City, Nev. Terr., 1868

N EVADA DESERVES A SPECIAL
niche in the journalism history of the Old West!
It was wild-and-wordy, intriguing and roisterous.

In 1863 Robert E. Draper of the *Aurora Times*
was crippled for life in a shotgun duel. In 1874
E. J. Parkinson of the *Nevada Tribune* and David
Sessions of the Carson City *Daily Appeal* shot
each others with revolvers to climax an editorial
feud. Reporter Alfred Chartz of the Eureka
Daily Republican killed a railroad conductor during an argument over something Chartz had
written. There were other duels, fisticuffs and
angry exchanges to lend spice to the mundane
chores of hand-spiking type or tugging at a press
lever.

(Opposite page) Nevada Historical Society

(Opposite page) The *Reese River Reveille*, the first Nevada paper to reach 100 years of continuous publication,
was started on May 16, 1863, in the predominantly Copperhead mining camp named after Austin, Texas. Ironically, William C. Phillips, the publisher, had been a
neighbor of Abraham Lincoln in Illinois. Through the
years the paper has had numerous owners and has been
produced "in absentia" from Reno, Tonopah and Washington, D.C. (Above) Early home of *The Nevada State
Herald* in Wells. (Below) A Carson City edition of Nevada's first paper.

On July 24, 1874, Reporter Roger Robinette of *The Cupel* was drowned when a flash flood roared down the Eureka canyon and smashed the plant of that tiny weekly. The famed *Territorial Enterprise* had production problems when the local constabulary chained a prisoner to its press for two and a half days. Political opponents tried to prevent publication of *The Advertiser* in Ione by stealing the press lever. The editor saved the day by cutting a piece of mountain mahogany to replace the missing part.

To say the least, newspapering in the early encampments of Nevada was exhilerating, a mite dangerous and as unpredictable as the ore lodes which indirectly spawned the historic gazettes.

Journalism in the Silver State can be traced back to "about 1854." A tiny hand-written sheet —the *Gold Canyon Switch* — was produced in Johntown, Utah Territory, by Joseph Webb, a partner of "Old Virginy" (Finney) Fenimore, after whom Virginia City was later named. A

This spindly Linotype marked the end of the hand-set era for the *Territorial Enterprise*. Strangely enough, Mark Twain, who adopted his famous pseudonym while working for the same paper, lost a small fortune by investing in a mechanical typesetting apparatus which did not have the success of Mergenthaler's machine.

Sketch courtesy of Harold's Club, Reno

second manuscript paper—*The Scorpion*—first came from the pen of Stephen A. Kinsey on February 1, 1857, at Genoa. That tiny settlement in the Carson River Valley was originally known as Mormon Station, and it was here that Nevada's first printed paper came into being.

While gold had already been discovered in the region, W. L. Jernegan and Alfred James arrived in Genoa with a printing press before the boom. The village was a freighters' way-point between California and Deseret—and its potential as a newspaper town was limited indeed. Nonetheless, on December 18, 1858, the two optimistic newsmen pulled Volume I, No. 1 of the *Territorial Enterprise* off their trusty hand-press.

In spite of its unlikely locale, the paper survived its shaky start. Before the end of its first year, however, the *Enterprise* was appearing with a Carson City dateline. That same summer the unexpected happened! Gold and silver were discovered in unbelievable quantities in the Washoe country, and the Comstock Lode trans-

(Above) On April 19, 1879, the *Eureka Sentinel* experienced its second disastrous fire. Legend has it that the paper went to press the very next day, while the building was still smoldering and the press almost too hot to touch. Typesetters had to be doused with water to keep from collapsing. (Left) William J. Forbes brought a special spark to Nevada journalism both as an editor and as a paragrapher under the pen name "Semblins." Utah and California also shared his talents.

115

Whenever frontier journalism is mentioned, the name of Mark Twain invariably enters the conversation. While his period of service on the **Territorial Enterprise** and several early California papers was relatively brief, Samuel Langhorne Clemens became a legend in the annals of newspapering for his wit, his imagination and his personal habits. Young Sam learned to set type for his brother, Orion, a Missouri newspaper publisher. Later he wandered about the East as a teen-age itinerant printer.

In 1861 when Orion was named territorial secretary of Nevada, Sam accompanied his brother westward. Unsuccessfully, he tried his luck with a timber claim and then at mining. It was following the latter venture that he penned several humorous items for the **Territorial Enterprise,** s i g n i n g them as "Josh." The fresh satirical letters brought him an offer of a job for $25 a week, and he reportedly walked the 60 or 70 miles from the Esmeralda district to Virginia City and his date with destiny on the **Enterprise.**

He worked for that paper less than two years, but during that time he shaped the writing style which was to make him famous— and he adopted the pen name by which he is universally known.

formed the once fruitless region into an unparalleled bonanza-land.

When Virginia City developed as the belle of the new golconda, the *Territorial Enterprise* made its third and final move to more glittering pastures. Jernegan and James were gone, and another owner, Jonathan Williams, had the equipment hauled to the heart of the Comstock in October of 1860. Within a year it had become a daily, with the ownership ultimately passing to Joseph T. Goodman and Denis E. McCarthy. In the free-spending climate of Virginia City, the *Enterprise* was a whopping success. Goodman and McCarthy were supposed to have carried their daily cash revenues home in water buckets

—but it is doubtful if the paper ever reached the magnificent heights of power and pecuniary return ascribed to it by local legend.

No question about it, though, the *Territorial Enterprise*—whether by design or historical accident — attracted an array of talent seldom matched by other frontier journals. Joe Goodman was a publisher of exceptional ability. Dan De Quille (William Wright) favored the paper for almost four decades with his lucid pen, and it was he who brought out the most in a disgruntled prospector named Sam Clemens, who came to work for the *Enterprise* in 1862. Clemens had attracted attention by sending in several humorous sketches from the Esmeralda district which he simply signed "Josh." During his brief but flamboyant career on the *Enterprise,* he adopted his famous pen-name: Mark Twain.

Nevada's early-day newspaper talent wasn't limited to Virginia City, however. In Carson City Sam P. Davis, editor of the *Appeal,* created one of the West's strangest papers, the *Waubuska Mangler.* Actually, the *Mangler* was a figment of Davis's imagination. He had fictitious battles with the non-existent editor of the *Mangler,* whom he labeled a "disgrace to journalism." Davis maintained the hoax several years before he simply wrote it out of existence.

No story of Nevada journalism would be complete without a mention of William J. Forbes, who was the epitome of the wandering frontier editor. A puckish paragrapher, Forbes brightened the pages of numerous papers he either served or owned. His pen name—"Semblins"—was widely known, but somehow he never achieved the lasting fame which came to such contemporaries as Twain, Bret Harte and Bill Nye. He gave his papers such interesting titles as the *Measure for Measure* (Battle Mountain) and *The Daily Trespass* (Virginia City).

Nevada also had two of the youngest editors in Western journalism history. The Olcovich brothers—nine and eleven years old—published *The Sun* in Carson City in 1888. James W. E. (Lying Jim) Townsend kept his frontier readers laughing with his fabrications—murder trials, railroad accidents and city scandals which he concocted

(Above) Dan De Quille was Mark Twain's literary sidekick on the *Territorial Enterprise.* His real name was William Wright, but for almost 40 years he reported the affairs of Nevada and Virginia City sprightly and humorously under his pseudonym. Twain's senior by half a dozen years, De Quille reputedly helped the younger writer develop a style at the critical point in his career. They tippled together, perpetrated hoaxes together. Talented though he was, De Quille, with his Quaker upbringing, lacked the audacity to push his way to fame. (Below) This sketch by artist Paul Nyeland depicts the harried activity of press day in the office of the *Territorial Enterprise.*

The *Reno* Gazette was founded on March 28, 1876, by John F. Alexander when he was 23 years old. In the 1880s the tall tales of J. E. W. (Lying Jim) Townsend made it one of the most popular papers in the state.

Publisher Phil S. Triplett and his son, Charles, posed for this graphic photo in the editorial office of the *Nevada State Herald* in Wells. The vintage typewriter, the ever-ready paste pot and the mountain of exchanges typified newspapering in the small towns of the West. Some editors actually "wrote" more with a scissors and a jar of paste than they did with quill or the crude typewriters of the day. It was the custom to exchange editions with all neighboring papers—whether they were friend or foe—and many editors sent dozens of copies back East and even overseas. Clipping was a universal right, provided credit was given.

Husband-and-wife publishing teams were commonplace on the frontier. Before 1900 the women were more often found in the back shop rather than in editorial positions.

Mrs. Phil S. Triplett, shown here, helped her spouse by hand-spiking ads for the *Nevada State Herald* which was published right in their home.

right at the typecase on such papers as the Reno *Gazette* and the Carson City *Daily Index.* Then there was the press-less printer, J. A. Talbott, who brought Potosi its first paper in 1861, a manuscript sheet with the unwieldy title: *East of the Nevada; or the Miner's Voice from the Colorado.* In the same mining camp Capt. J. E. Stevens countered with his own unique hand - written paper, the *Potosi Nix Cum Rouscht.*

Newspapering in frontier Nevada was glorious and gaudy. Its editors tickled funny bones and vented speens. Unfortunately, success was tied to the wealth of the mines—and the mortality rate was high. Glamorous as it was, journalism in Nevada was not easy, and when Orlando E. Jones, a former circus clown, folded the Hawthorne *Oasis,* his final lament read: "It may be possible to publish a newspaper on one square meal a week; but to undertake to do so on one square a month . . . is a little more than human nature can stand."

Truly, all that glittered on the frontier was not gold!

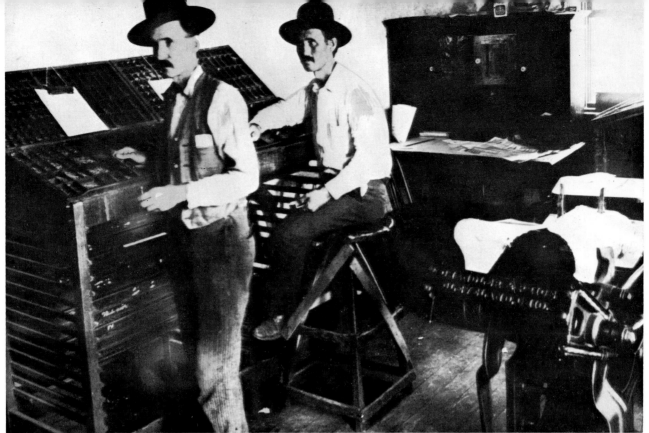

Oklahoma:

The Legacy of Sequoyah

(Above) Typesetters of *The Cherokee Advocate* at Tahlequah, Indian Territory. (Below) Sequoyah made Indian-language newspapers possible with his invention of the 85-character Cherokee Alphabet.

"Some people think because they subscribe for a paper and pay for it, the editor is thereby under obligations to write especially for them, and when they see anything in it that doesn't exactly suit their views they pronounce the paper a fraud and the editor an ass."

Oklahoma Star
January 4, 1876

To UNDERSTAND THE DEVELOPMENT of journalism in Oklahoma, it is necessary to have at least a casual knowledge of that state's unusual history. During the exciting years when other areas were experiencing gold rushes, the advent of the railroads, boomerism and the high tide of homesteading, the land that is now Oklahoma was Indian Territory.

As the western terminus of the Trail of Tears, it became the treaty-protected home of the Five Civilized Tribes and other displaced Indians. Under the watchful eye of the U. S. Cavalry, the

(Opposite page) Frontier journalism had advanced to great heights when this picture was taken of the *Woods County Enterprise*. In addition to pulley-driven presses, the shop boasted electric lights for its compositors.

Oklahoma Historical Society

(Above) Schools in the Indian Territory recognized the importance of printing, and both boys and girls received training. As early as 1848, a school newspaper—*The Cherokee Rosebud*—was published by students of Park Hill Female Seminary. (Below) Sequoyah's Cherokee syllabary. (Below right) Guthrie, the capital of Oklahoma Territory, literally grew up over night. This shack housed its first printing office.

Muriel H. Wright

region was off-limits to white settlers and hustlers, thus setting the stage for the great land rushes of 1889 and later years.

The Cherokees, Creeks, Chickasaws, Choctaws and Seminoles who made up the Five Civilized Tribes were not the cliche-Indians of Hollywood. Before the tragic removals to the western lands, they had advanced to socio-economic levels unheard of among other tribes to the north and west. Many of their leaders were college-trained; some owned large plantations which were operated with slave labor; they developed teachers and tradesmen of outstanding ability.

On of these tradesmen was a crippled Cherokee silversmith named Sequoyah. In about 1809 he started developing a "talking leaf" for his people. Using bark, charcoal and an old English spelling book, he worked endlessly on his project. Many Indians scoffed at his idea; some thought him demented because of his preoccupation. In time, however, he created a syllabary of the Cherokee tongue, making it possible for written communication within the tribe.

So successful was his Cherokee Alphabet that it was ultimately cast into type. In 1828 *The Cherokee Phoenix*, the first Indian newspaper, was printed at New Echota, Georgia. This publication was the genesis of Oklahoma journalism. When the capital of the Cherokee Nation was re-established at Tahlequah, Indian Territory, *The Cherokee Advocate* was started as an outgrowth of the earlier *Phoenix*. A bi-lingual newspaper,

Oklahoma Historical Society

The Advocate was first issued on September 6, 1844. Its editor was William P. Ross, a mixed-blood Cherokee who had been educated at Princeton. Sequoyah, incidentally, never did see a copy of the Tahlequah paper. He died in Mexico the preceding year.

Actually *The Advocate* was preceded by another publication, *The Cherokee Messenger,* first produced at the Cherokee Baptist Mission in August of 1844. Because of its format, irregular-ity of issue and emphasis on religious material, *The Messenger* has not been recognized as a true newspaper, thus precluding its acceptance as Oklahoma's first.

The Five Civilized Tribes proved their advanced culture by following these first gazettes with a number of excellent frontier newspapers. *The Indian Journal* published at Muskogee carried news in both English and Creek. *The Choctaw Telegraph, The Choctaw Intelligencer* and

(Above) Researchers used this faded photo of a pioneer territorial newspaper office to achieve realism in the movie "Cimarron." (Below) A sketch of the second press to produce *The Cherokee Advocate.* (Right) The first print-shop in Clinton, Oklahoma Territory.

(Below) Thomas Gilcrease Institute

CHEROKEE MESSENGER.

ᏣᎳᎩ ᎠᏰᎵ.

VOL. I.   SEPTEMBER, 1844.   NO. 2.

Translation of Genesis into the Cherokee Language.

(Cherokee syllabary text reproduced in the newspaper image.)

University of Oklahoma Bulletin

Division of Manuscripts, Library, University of Oklahoma

(Above left) *The Cherokee Messenger*, which was printed in Sequoyah's alphabet, came out in August of 1844, a month earlier than *The Cherokee Advocate*. However, most researchers do not consider it a true newspaper. (Above right) *The Minco Minstrel* was one of many journals started after the opening of Indian Territory. (Below left) Henry P. Robbins, editor of the *McAlester News-Capitol*. (Below right) *The Democrat* was Ponca City's first newspaper. It was housed in the frame building in the background.

Division of Manuscripts, Library, University of Oklahoma

The Chickasaw and Choctaw Herald all preceded the Civil War. It was an era unparalleled in American journalism history.

With secession and the outbreak of hostilities, many Indian leaders—in person and through their newspapers—urged tribesmen to adopt a "hands-off" policy as far as the war was concerned. But once again the cruel hand of fate dealt a circum-

Oklahoma Historical Society

Territorial newspaper plants in Oklahoma were much the same as others throughout the West. They were generally cluttered, poorly lighted, ill-heated and notoriously unat- **tractive. Equipment usually consisted of a stone, a few cases of type, a job press and a cylinder. This backshop of *The Minco Minstrel* was typical.**

stantial blow to the Indians. Because of the proximity to Confederate States, the presence of numerous Southern agents, the withdrawal of Federal troops from the territory and the fact that some of the wealthier Indians once were slaveholders, it became a common belief in the North that the Indians were sympathetic to the South. This was in spite of the fact that many of them fought consistently for the Union.

At the war's end, the philosophy that the Indians had lost their rights by supporting the Confederacy was advanced by land-hungry whites seeking to abrogate the treaty responsibilities. The results were not immediate, but gradually the pressures mounted until it became only a matter of time before the Indian Territory would be opened to settlement.

Meanwhile, in the post-war years the tribes

continued to develop their schools, their communities and their newspapers. The *Indian Chieftain, Our Brother in Red, The Indian Arrow* and *The Tahlequah Telephone* were among the chronicles started in the pre-opening era. In layout, format and editorial content these and other Indian papers were much like their counterparts elsewhere in the West. Editors were not above verbal scalpings, and inter-paper rivalries were as fiery as those in any other region. One, in fact, resulted in a murder.

B. H. Stone, editor of *The Tahlequah Telephone,* wrote heated criticisms of *The Cherokee Advocate.* The differences between Brown and E. C. Boudinot, Jr., then editor of *The Advocate,* grew so bitter that on October 1, 1887, Boudinot walked into his rival's office and gunned him down with a .45.

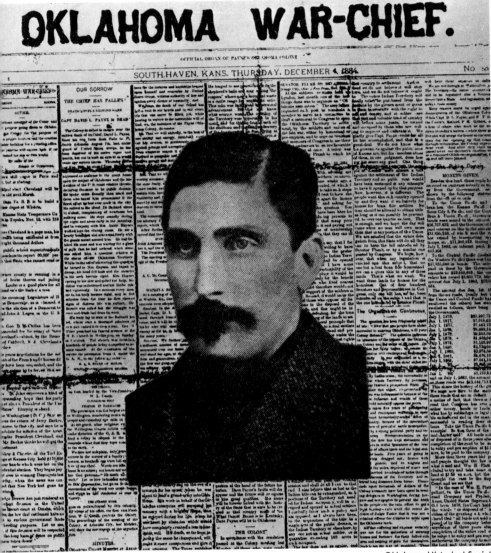

OKLAHOMA WAR-CHIEF.

OFFICIAL ORGAN OF PAYNE'S OKLAHOMA COLONY.

SOUTH.HAVEN. KANS. THURSDAY. DECEMBER 4, 1884.   No 50

Oklahoma Historical Society

David L. Payne, a distant cousin of Davey Crockett, was the most famous of the "Boomers" who sought the opening of the "Unassigned Lands" in Indian Territory. A Civil War veteran and former member of the Kansas legislature, Payne organized numerous colonies of hopeful settlers anxious to claim homesteads in Oklahoma. To promote his aims, he established his own newspaper, known at various times as the **Oklahoma Chief** and the **Oklahoma War-Chief.**

Like Payne's basic enterprise, the newspaper was illegal and thus led a turbulent and hectic life. Successive issues were seldom published in the same place after the first edition came off the press on January 12, 1883, at Caldwell, Kansas. Payne tried to keep one jump ahead of Federal authorities, but in the summer of 1884, he was overtaken. In attempting to establish the town of Rock Falls in the Cherokee Strip, the "Boomers" were evicted by a detachment of Negro troops. Their leader was arrested and the newspaper plant destroyed. Payne was ultimately released, but he died on November 28, 1884, before he could organize another colony. The **War - Chief** continued for two more years, advocating the opening of "Oklahoma Lands" which finally occurred in 1889.

Stone died a few hours after the shooting and the next edition of *The Telephone* was issued by his widow who reversed the column rules on Page 2, the era's symbol of bereavement.

After the Civil War the Creeks and Seminoles ceded an unoccupied tract in the heart of Indian Territory which became known popularly as "Oklahoma Lands." By 1880 an intense campaign was begun to have this area opened to homesteading. Against the law, cattlemen from Kansas grazed their herds over vast areas of Indian Territory. Ever-increasing numbers of "Boomers" gathered on the border and made repeated attempts to colonize the "Unassigned Lands," only to be driven out by Federal troops. In 1886-87 the Atchison, Topeka & Sante Fe Railroad was built across the area.

The culmination came on April 22, 1889, when the first mad Run was authorized. Within 24 hours about 50,000 settlers poured into the territory. These included many "Sooners" who sneaked in ahead of the starting signal to select choice plots. Printers and editors were not far behind, and as soon as tents or frame shacks could be erected, newspapers were underway. In Guthrie (which became the capital when Oklahoma Territory was established in 1890), the *Guthrie Getup* appeared just a week after the Run with this pronouncement: "Praise God all ye good people, and let these prairies resound to the measured strokes of our job press. Ah, there is the rub, if you do not give us job work, we will have to go back to our wife's folks. This would place us in a h--- of a fix, as we are not married. Our

last statement is especially directed to single ladies who hold corner lots . . ."

Other gazettes soon followed. The *Oklahoma Times* emerged from a tent in Oklahoma City. An earlier paper, the *Oklahoma City Times,* had been printed irregularly at Wichita and Purcell before the first Run. Most of its copies went to eastern readers. Other newspapers and other Runs followed, and the erosion of the once sprawling Indian Territory reached its peak.

While Oklahoma did not officially become a state until 1907, the development toward that goal was rapid after the initial opening. Newspapers played a vital role throughout the transition—but with the passing of the Indian Press, one of the most romantic chapters in western journalism came to an end.

(Above) Like many territorial newspapers, the *Anadarko Democrat* was born in unimpressive quarters. This tent-covered frame construction was commonplace during the first days of the great land rushes. (Right) At Atoka in the Choctaw Nation, *The Indian Champion* was first published in 1884 without a nameplate. Later it was called the *Branding Iron* because of the great number of cattle brand advertisements it carried.

Oregon:

The Invective Was Infectious

"Gentlemen, dig up the stumps, grade the streets, tax dogs, prohibit hogs—and advertise in the Spectator."

Oregon Spectator
Oregon City, Feb. 5, 1846

ODDLY ENOUGH, NEWSPAPERS WERE flourishing at the end of the trail before they appeared along the way. "Oregon" was a magic word to thousands of restless souls in the East and Midwest. Unlike other meccas of the frontier, however, Oregon did not offer the sudden riches of gold and silver. Hers was a beckoning of hope, of a "new life," of lush valleys and of freedom— as each individual interpreted it.

While only adventurous men and a few women of doubtful repute hit the gold trails, families made the trek to Oregon. From the beginning there was more stability along the Willamette River than in the glittering gulches of Eldorado. It was a place to build homes, to plan cities and to start newspapers.

(Opposite page) Eugene Register-Guard (Robert B. Frazier)

(Opposite page) The Eugene *Guard* was established in 1867 and survived the rigors of the early decades to become the *Register-Guard*. (Above) The famed Spalding missionary press of Lapwai, Idaho, came to Oregon to produce the state's third paper, the *Oregon American and Evangelical Unionist*. George H. Himes, publisher and newspaper historian, is on the right. (Below) During its infancy, the *Oregonian* was housed in this tiny building next to the home of Thomas J. Dryer, its editor.

129

Oregon Historical Society

Like many other "first" newspapers, the **Oregon Spectator** was relatively short-lived. While it existed, however, it was a robust little sheet which tackled the problems of the day. Typical of frontier journals, it carried a minimum of local news. Its editor, W. G. T'Vault, was a lawyer, not a newspaperman. This was not an unusual arrangement; throughout the Old West attorneys were prominent in the affairs of journalism.

Modern techniques of reporting were unknown. In spite of the limited size of the paper (four pages, 11½x17 inches over all) there was little attempt at brevity. Twice a month the **Spectator** came out with rambling discourses on a wide variety of subjects. A la Benjamin Franklin, it carried such self-help advice as the following: "If you have no wife, get one; if you have, God bless her, stay at home with her, instead of spending your evenings with expensive fooleries."

The West Coast's first newspaper was printed on a Washington hand-press by John Fleming—before he rushed off to the California gold fields. At the height of the paper's popularity, its circulation reached a mere 155. It lasted from February 5, 1846, until it was suspended in March of 1855. The Oregon Printing Association which started the **Spectator** adhered to a strongly non-partisan viewpoint. This caused a rapid turnover in editors. George L. Curry, the third man to take up the quill, wrote a final editorial blasting press censorship when he was dismissed. Despite such limitations, however, the **Oregon Spectator** deserves a hallowed spot in the annals of frontier journalism.

Great Britain and the United States were still bickering over the region when a small group of Oregon City business men formed the Oregon Printing Association in late 1845. This organization was an outgrowth of the Pioneer Lyceum and Literary Club whose members had consider-

able interest in the political issues of the day. A newspaper, they reasoned, would help them "promote science, temperance, morality and general intelligence," so they ordered a Washington hand-press shipped to them from New York.

On February 5, 1846, the *Oregon Spectator* be-

Oregon Historical Society

came a reality. The editor was W. G. T'Vault, a lawyer who took the job for $300 a year—which was $250 more than he got for being postmaster general of the provisional government. The printer was John Fleming.

At least a year before the *Spectator* hit the streets, Oregon City had another sheet which didn't quite qualify as a regular newspaper. It had the unusual and intriguing title of *Flumgudgeon Gazette and Bumble Bee Budget.* "Devoted to scratching and stinging the follies of the times" was the avowed purpose of the tiny manuscript paper which was published anonymously by someone who called himself Curltail Coon. The dateline noted the place of publication as Flumgudgeonburg. Years later a former Oregon City business man—Charles Edward Pickett—claimed to have been the mysterious Mr. Coon.

Oregon City's second printed newspaper, the *Free Press,* was published by 28-year-old George L. Curry, who had edited the *Spectator* for a time and later was to become governor. With no press available to him, Curry commissioned Victor M.

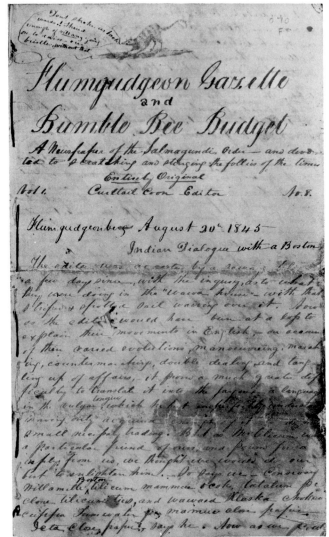

(Above) Floods and fires were hard on Oregon newspapers. The latter were particularly disastrous, wiping out many invaluable files. This crowd gathered in front of the Oregon City *Enterprise* office was watching the receding waters of the 1890 flood. (Right) The *Flumgudgeon Gazette and Bumble Bee Budget* was a manuscript paper in Oregon City before the advent of the *Spectator.* It spoofed the people and affairs of the day in English and Chinook jargon. Its editor was anonymous.

Oregon Historical Society

(Above) Portland, like other major centers in the West, has had scores of papers since the *Oregonian* was founded in 1850. Many were small special-interest publications like the *Oregon Native Son*. (Below) A rugged old Ramage press which saw historic service in Oregon.

Oregon Historical Society

Wallace, a machinist, to build one on the scene. In his first issue, the editor wrote: "Although it is made of wood, Mr. W. thinks it will be able to tell the truth quite as well as an iron one."

Curry had another problem, too. The worn old font of French Didot type he got from Catholic missionaries was short of w's, so the editor had to resort to double v's and some makeshift letters he supposedly carved out of hardwood. All in all, it was a lot of work to produce a paper which only lasted for six months. The first issue came out on April 8, 1848. By late summer the California gold rush was luring potential subscribers (and typesetters) southward in droves. It wiped the *Free Press* out of business, while the *Spectator* was shut down for more than a month. The latter apologized thusly:

"The *Spectator* after a temporary sickness greets its patrons and hopes to serve them faithfully. . . . That 'gold fever' which has swept about 3,000 of the officers, lawyers, physicians, farmers, and mechanics of Oregon into the mines of California, took away our printer also . . ."

The *Spectator* folded for good in March of

132

(Above) In its first years *The Oregon Statesman* was a peripatetic journal which followed the territorial capital from Oregon City to Salem to Corvallis and back to Salem where it remained and prospered. (Below left) Asahel Bush, the fiery-pen editor of *The Statesman,* was one of Oregon's most influential and certainly most out-spoken newspapermen. More than any other writer, he helped create the so-called "Oregon style" with his vituperative, no-holds-barred editorials. He later became a respected, successful banker. (Below right) This building in Salem housed *The Oregon Statesman* as well as the short-lived *Oregon Vidette and Antimonopolist.*

1855 but during its existence its press produced a broadside which set the stage for some harum-scarum personal journalism to follow. The inflammatory flyer was written by James W. Nesmith, vice president of the Oregon Printing Association and a U.S. Senator-to-be. It read:

"TO THE WORLD!!—J. Quinn Thornton, having resorted to low, cowardly and dishonorable means, for the purpose of injuring my character and standing, and having refused honorable satisfaction, which I have demanded; I avail myself of this opportunity of publishing him to the world

as a reclaimless liar, an infamous scoundrel, a worthless vagabond and an imported micreant, a disgrace to the profession and a dishonor to his country."

Although this statement appeared on a broadside rather than in an actual newspaper, it was a forerunner of a free-swinging brand of personal journalism which came to be called the "Oregon Style." Actually, all the western states had editors who wrote in this libel-be-damned fashion, but Oregon had the jump on most of them, so it wa simply a matter of first there, first tarnished!

Three prominent editors helped created the so-called "style." The first was Thomas Jefferson Dryer, who came from California with his Ramage press to print Portland's first paper, the *Weekly Oregonian,* a Whig journal. Several months later—in March of 1851—*The Oregon Statesman,* a Democratic sheet, was launched by irascible Asahel Bush in Oregon City. Some time later, pugnacious W. L. Adams purchased the plant of the defunct *Spectator* for $1,200 and

began to publish the *Oregon Argus,* a distinctively Republican organ.

That trio stirred up a seething cauldron of editorial invective which left their readers gasping. The running battle between Dryer and Bush was especially caustic. They pulled no punches in degrading one another and their respective newspapers. No winner was crowned, but there is a general concensus among researchers that Bush had less qualms about the level of his attacks. In one issue he wrote about Dryer: "We cannot get down to the depths he has sunk to answer him, for we will not sully our columns with vulgarity and slang."

Not long afterwards he penned:

"There is not a brothel in the land that would not have felt itself disgraced by the presence of the *Oregonian* of week before last. It was a complete tissue of gross profanity, obscenity, falsehood, and meanness. And yet it was but little below the standard of that characterless sheet."

(Below left) The *Bedrock Democrat,* founded in 1870, was the first newspaper in Baker, a robust mining center. One of the founders was L. L. McArthur, an ex-Confederate army officer. *The Daily Sage Brush* first appeared in 1883;

Oregon State Archives

it withered away within five years. (Below right) In Salem Will H. Parry started the *Capital Journal* in 1888 as a Republican sheet. It was published in this building which it shared with the postoffice.

Cronise Studio

Who said frontier editors didn't have any fun?

While Oregon publishers fought mostly with words, there was some physical violence, too. In 1871, for instance, William Thompson, 23-year-old editor of the Roseburg *Plaindealer,* was caned and shot by Henry and Thomas Gale, who published the competitive *Ensign.* Firing in return, Thompson killed Henry Gale.

Newspapering in Oregon, as it developed, had a little bit of everything. It had gold camp ga-

(Above) Union membership had more social and fraternal implications around the turn of the century. This was the Portland Pressmen's Union prior to a parade. (Right) Cincinnatus Hiner (Joaquin) Miller, the "poet of the Sierras," started his career in Oregon. In 1858-59 he attended Columbia College in Eugene, being admitted to the Oregon bar a year later. In 1860 Miller became editor of the *Democratic Herald* in Eugene, a paper which changed names periodically to avoid suspension by the federal government for its pro-Confederacy editorials. While in Eugene he also wrote an article defending the Mexican brigand, Joaquin Murietta, whose given name he later adopted as his own. Before he went on to greater fame as a poet, he was a judge in Canyon City where he was a contributor to the *City Journal.*

Jacksonville Museum, Southern Oregon Historical Society

Medford became southern Oregon's leading city when the railroad by-passed Jacksonville, at that time the news center of the rich mining region. In 1887 Medford got its first newspaper, the *Monitor*. A year later the *Mail* was started by Thomas Harlan. This is the back shop of the old *Mail Tribune*, which was formed through the merger of the city's second paper and the *Medford Tribune*, originally established in Ashland.

zettes, a few boomer sheets when the railroads came in and those which profiteered on timber claims and land notice legals. There were Oregon newspapers like the Madras *Pioneer* published in tents. The Bend *Bulletin* first came off a press in a log hut. The *Harney Valley Items* topped them all, however, being published in a former house of ill-repute. In Halsey a barber ran a paper as a side line. The *Northwestern* of Klamath Falls fell on hard times and passed from the sheriff to the coroner who named a couple of deputies to run it. When things got tough in 1890, the *Harney Press* reflected:

"In order to get a little ready cash the editor of the *Press* has been teaching school, the junior editor of the *Herald* is waiting on table at the Burns hotel, and the editor of the *Items* says he is looking for a soft job sawing wood."

University of Oregon Library

(Right) The prospectus of *The Roseburg Ensign*. The Gale brothers who published it got into a fatal shooting scrape with William (Bud) Thompson of the rival *P l a i n d e a l e r*. (Left) W. G. T'Vault was Oregon's first editor. After the *Spectator*, he operated the *Table Rock Sentinel* and the *Intelligencer*, both in Jacksonville. When the latter paper proved unsuccessful, he returned to the practice of law, his original profession.

PROSPECTUS
OF
The Roseburg Ensign.

On or before the first day of May, 1867, the undersigned propose to commence the publication of a weekly newspaper, at Roseburg, Douglas county, Oregon, to be entitled THE ROSEBURG ENSIGN. We have been induced to enter upon this enterprise for several reasons: First—The interests and importance of the Umpqua Valley demand the services of a local organ, devoted to the development of the varied resources of this section of our State. To make the ENSIGN a faithful and reliable advocate of these interests shall be our earnest and constant aim. We shall at all times endeavor to furnish our readers with a correct record of current local events and general and State news.

Politically the ENSIGN will be an uncompromising advocate of the principles and policy of the Union party.

In connection with our office we shall have material for doing all kinds of job printing.

Persons receiving a copy of this prospectus are respectfully solicited to act as agent in obtaining subscribers for the ENSIGN.

M. & H. H. GALE.

Terms $3.00 per annum in advance

136

Eugene Register-Guard

Oregon journalism had its characters, too, not the least of whom was John W. (Watermelon) Redington. Colonel Redington was an Indian fighter, prospector, humorist and eccentric. In 1883 when he was publishing in eastern Oregon, he promoted his paper by painting signs on rocks and fences all over the country side. A typical example: "The *Heppner Gazette*—Hell on Horse Thieves and Hypocrites."

Earlier, an editor of *The Statesman* in Salem, Redington described some of the problems of newspapering in early Oregon:

"I used to rustle ads for the four-page paper, but it was worse than painful dentistry, and when I tried to collect bills, I invited getting shot, or at least half-shot. So I got scared . . . joined the army and went scouting through three Indian wars, thus getting into the safety zone."

That sort of forthrightness characterized the early papers of the 33rd state, from the Amity *Popgun* to the mellifluous "*Oregon Irrigator* of Irrigon, Oregon." The heritage of the tiny *Spectator*—short-lived as it was—gave editors something to build on!

In 1867 the Eugene *Guard* was established by J. B. Alexander, who operated it for a year before turning it over to J. W. Skaggs. The latter ran into financial difficulties and reputedly passed it on to William (Bud) Thompson with this comment: "If you will take it, I will give you not only the Washington hand-press and the type, but two bundles of paper and two cords of wood." The photos on this page are of the *Guard* back shop some time around the turn of the century.

Eugene Register-Guard

Texas-New Mexico

Nacogdoches Leads the Way

"We promise the public of our beloved country that our press will never cease its operation till our silence shall announce to them that there is no longer in Texas a resting place for a free press. . ."

Telegraph and Texas Register
Galveston, 1836

Before most of the other western states had experienced their first small trickle of settlers, Texas boasted almost half a hundred newspapers. In 1813 journalism in the Old West had its birth at Nacogdoches. At that time Texas was still part of Spanish America, and the brief era of the filibusterer had begun.

A small two-column sheet, the *Gaceta de Texas,* was printed in Natchitoches, Louisiana, but it carried a date line which read: "Nacogdoches, 25 de Mayo, de 1813." That same year another paper,

(Opposite page) A Texas newspaper could hardly have a more appropriate name than *The Lone Star,* published in El Paso by S. N. Newman. The year of this photo was 1882. (Above) *The Galveston News* has been in business since April 11, 1842, when Texas was a republic. This is a sketch of one of its early homes. (Below) Newspapering in the 17 states of the Old West had its beginning in Nacogdoches, Texas. In 1813—when Spanish dominion was being challenged by the filibusterers—the *Gaceta de Texas,* though printed in Natchitoches, Louisiana, carried a Nacogdoches dateline.

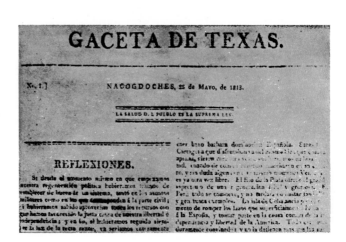

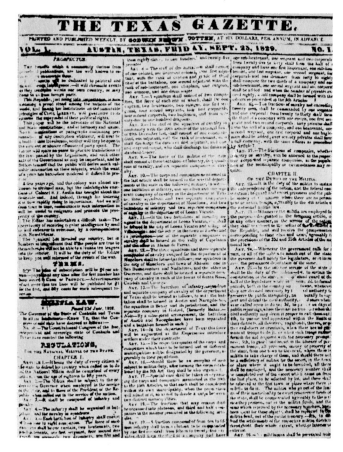

El Mejicano, was being produced in Nacogdoches by José Alvarez de Toledo. These were revolutionary publications of short duration, but until some new evidence is found, they pre-date all other journalistic efforts in the 17 western states.

Six years later, when Dr. James Long—last of the filibusterers—made his abortive effort to oust the Spanish, he also established a newspaper in Nacogdoches. His *Texas Republican,* which was edited by Horatio Biglow, was used primarily to promote sympathy for his mission in the United States.

The value of the press as a tool of revolution continued in Texas for more than two decades. Mexico had broken free of Spanish domination in 1821, and in the process she had inherited the problems of her unruly northern province. When Santa Anna's forces invaded Texas, the crisis brought forth one of the Lone Star State's most

Willard Richardson (above left) directed *The Galveston News* from 1844 to 1875, through the difficult years of the Civil War and Reconstruction. (Top) *The True Blue* was a tiny manuscript paper published in 1842 by irrepressible Texans in a Mexican prison. (Bottom) This is Volume I, Number 1 of *The Texas Gazette* which first appeared in San Felipe de Austin in September of 1829. Godwin Brown Cotton was its publisher.

famous and courageous journals: the *Telegraph and Texas Register*.

The paper's impassioned publisher was Gail Borden, who was to go on to greater wealth and recognition in the milk industry. But in 1835 he thought only of the invading hordes from Mexico. His paper was a year old when the massacre at the Alamo Mission occurred. From its columns the report of the disaster was reprinted by other editors throughout the U.S. In a banner headline, Borden blazoned the historical slogan: "Remember the Alamo!"

When the Mexican army advanced on San Felipe —where Borden had been printing the *Telegraph and Register*—the publisher moved his plant to Harrisburg. Santa Anna caught up with him there and destroyed his press. Yet Borden and his associates persisted; they found another press and moved to Galveston where the paper continued to harass the enemy and to enlist support from the north.

It was also in the same city—four years before the *Oregon Spectator* appeared — that Samuel Bangs established *The Galveston News* on April 11, 1842, under the flag of the Republic of Texas. Bangs was a colorful character who in the past

(Above) When frontier towns grew more populated, job printing plants were established away from the newspaper offices. This was Ford & Bedford's Job Shop in Dallas. (Right) Ingenious Gail Borden, who became famous for his revolutionary condensed milk process, was publisher of the *Telegraph and Texas Register* in 1835. It boldly fostered Texas independence from Mexico.

(Below) Division of Manuscripts, Library, University of Oklahoma

(Above) University of Texas Library

had been associated with the notorious Jean Lafitte. Shortly before Texas was annexed to the U.S. in 1845, *The News* came under the editorial control of Willard Richardson, a dynamic frontier editor who directed the paper for more than 30 years. By 1855 *The News* had a "power" press—operated quite uniquely by a blind horse walking on a treadmill.

During the Civil War Richardson escaped Union forces in Galveston by moving his operation to Houston. There he was burned out, but still he survived, moving back to Galveston to carry on scathing editorial attacks on the scalawags and carpet-baggers of the Reconstruction Period. In 1885 *The Galveston News* acquired *The Dallas Herald* (founded in 1849) and created another paper, *The Dallas Morning News*, which like its namesake became a prosperous, modern daily.

Meanwhile, other chronicles appeared across the expansive width and breadth of Texas. As early as 1829 San Felipe de Austin had *The Texas Gazette,* published by Godwin Brown Cotton. In

(Above) In Texas the ten-gallon hats were worn on the range and not in the print shops. This is the office of the *Hubbard City News,* circa 1900. (Left) William Ransom (seated) and Frank Caldwell model what the well-dressed reporters wore in San Antonio in the 1880s.

142

1842 Texas imprisoned in Mexico issued a most unusual manuscript paper: *The True Blue.* That same year at Clarksville, Colonel Charles De Morse (often called the "father of Texas journalism") issued his *Northern Standard,* for which he accepted lard, tallow, beeswax and other products for payment.

Capsuling the scope of frontier newspapering in Texas on a few pages is a virtual impossibility. The saga is alive with sparkling characters like William Cowper Brann, whose facile pen brightened the Waco *Iconoclast;* Indian fighter and editor, Colonel John S. (Rip) Ford, who supposedly got his nickname from signing "R.I.P." ("Rest in Peace") on letters he wrote to survivors of battle victims; a convicted embezzler and tippler named Sidney William Porter, who failed as editor of a humorous weekly in Austin but who became famous as O. Henry.

There was violence (Brann was killed in a pistol fight with an irate reader); there was hardship (many sheets were produced on wallpaper; wrapping paper and old bills of lading); there was dogged courage under five different flags and two languages.

The Spanish-Mexican influence was also felt in the early days of journalism in New Mexico, too. That state's first paper, *El Crepusculo de la Libertad (The Dawn of Liberty),* was a tiny Spanish-language journal published in Taos on November 29, 1834, by Father Antonio Martinez and Printer Jesus Maria Baca. The same press—supposedly a Ramage—later produced *La Verdad (The Truth),* a Sante Fe weekly, and *The Republican,* the state's first English paper which appeared in the capital city in 1847. Two decades later drunken cowboys broke up the old press and threw it into the Cimarron River, when the editor of *The Cimarron News and Press* criticized their Saturday night revelries.

Editors in New Mexico fired editorial blasts with the best of them. One of the most outspoken was Charles L. Kusz, Jr., editor of *The Gringo & Greaser* at Manzano in 1884. He printed his little three-column paper entirely in italic type and alternately lambasted the Catholic Church and local cattle rustlers. He made many enemies, one of whom shot him to death at 35.

Generally, early-day journalism in the rugged, sun-burnt Southwest was much the same as elsewhere on the frontier. It was no place for a dude or dandy!

(Above) *The San Antonio Express* was typical of post-Civil War newspapers. Lack of headline type resulted in gray, unimaginative front pages. (Below) The sparsely populated areas of New Mexico were not as conducive to frontier newspapering as were other more settled communities throughout the Old West. Still, the early Mexican outposts, mining camps and railroad towns boasted journals printed in English, Spanish or sometimes a little of each. The state's first paper was printed in Taos in 1834. The plaza scene below shows the office of *The Sun* in Socorro in 1882.

Utah:

A Saga of Devils and Saints

"Printing is an art, and cannot be managed by every ignoramus who takes it into his head to start a newspaper."

The Wasatch Wave
Heber, Utah Terr., 1889

THE DOMINANCE OF MORMONISM in the creation and development of Utah was equally evident in the early newspaper history of Deseret.

This dominance was not stifling, however, because Brigham Young and the Council of Twelve were firm believers in the printing press. On the other hand, Utah in her youthful days was not the most comfortable locale for an anti-Mormon or a non-Mormon editor.

When the westward exodus to the Great Basin began, there was no printing equipment in the vanguard. But from the leadership came this exhortation: ". . . bring us the materials, where-

The sketch above depicts the excitement of publication day of the *Deseret News.* After 17 years as a weekly and semi-weekly, it finally appeared as a daily on November 20, 1867. (Opposite page) The old Deseret Store and Tithing Office in which the print shop was located for a time. (Below) Earlier the paper was published in this little adobe structure known as "Bullock's Money Mill." It had been used in 1849 to mint coins for the Saints.

DESERET NEWS.

BY W. RICHARDS.   G. S. L. CITY, DESERET, JUNE 15, 1850.   VOL. 1. - - NO. 1.

LAT. 40° 45' 44"   LON. 111° 26' 34"

PROSPECTUS.
DESERET NEWS.

MOTTO—"TRUTH AND LIBERTY."

We propose to publish a small weekly sheet, as large as our local circumstances will permit, to be called "*Deseret News*," de-

Companies of 20, and upwards, entered at once, 20 cents each.

A paper that is worth printing, is worth preserving; if worth preserving, it is worth binding; for this purpose we issue in pamphlet form; and if every subscriber shall preserve each copy of the "News," and bind it at the close of the volume, their children's children may

people, want the Union peacefully dissolved, why not dissolve it? Why ask Congress to do a thing they have no power to do? Congress did not make the Union; the Union made Congress, and the people made the Union; consequently, on the principles of federal republicanism, the same power that makes must unmake, if un-

Utah State Historical Society

ⱭⱮƧᴏᵻᴛ ꝂⱮᴏᴦᴎᵹ Ᏸᴨᴏ.   3

Ɣ ɑⱮƧᴏᵻᴛᴎ ᴊᴌᴘᴇᴃᴌᴆ Ɣ

			Letter.	Name.	Sound.
Long Sounds.			ꝛ		p
Letter.	Name.	Sound.	Ꝗ		ꝗ
ꝺ	e	as in eat.	ꝗ		t
Ɛ	a " ate.		ꝺ		d
ꝸ	ah " art.		C		che as in *cheese*.
ꝋ	aw " aught.		Ꝯ		g
O	o " oat.		ꝏ		k
Φ	oo " ooze.		ꝍ		ga as in *gate*.
Short Sounds of the above.			ᴘ		f
ꝉ	as in it.		ᴃ		v
ᴊ	" et.		ʟ		eth as in *thigh*.
ᴊ	" at.		ꝩ		the " *thy*
ꝡ	" ot.		ꝗ		s
ᴦ	" ut.		ꝺ		z
ꝯ	" book.		ꝺ		esh as in *flesh*.
Double Sounds.			Ꝧ		zhe " vision.
ꝺ	i as in ice.		ᴪ		ur " burn.
ꝺ	ow " owl.		ꝉ		l
ꝩ	ye		ꝺ		m
ꝟ	woo		ꝋ		n
ꝼ	h		ᴎ		eng as in *length*.

The proposed Mormon alphabet from "The Deseret First Reader," 1868, never quite caught on with the people.

Courtesy Deseret News

(Above) Vol. 1, No. 1 of the *Deseret News* was dated June 15, 1850, but the first impression was made, according to Mormon history, at 5:20 p.m. on the previous day. (Below) This painting by Paul S. Clowes depicts the pulling of the first copy of the *News* from the small Ramage. At the historic event, left to right, were Brigham H. Young, pressman; Horace K. Whitney, typesetter; Thomas Bullock, proof-reader, and Willard Richards, editor. The newspaper had been delayed several months while Brigham H. Young, the Mormon leader's nephew, set type for official documents.

Courtesy Deseret News

Geological Survey, The National Archives

(Above) *The Daily Reporter*, founded at Corinne in 1869, was a Gentile publication, and early in his career, Editor James H. Beadle was severely mauled by "fiendish Mormons"—as he described them—for his editorial comments. (Below) *The Mormon Tribune*, established in Salt Lake City, was the organ for a Reform Movement in the Church and was, therefore, extremely controversial. Later it dropped the word "Mormon" and became the *Salt Lake Tribune*, at the same time softening its avowed fight in behalf of "the priest-ridden people of Utah."

Utah State Historical Society

by we can furnish our children with books, and the Saints with new things to feast the soul."

With that command, William Wines Phelps, a Church printer in ill-fated Nauvoo, was authorized to go East to buy a press for the printing needs of the colony on the Great Salt Lake. The Ramage press which Phelps acquired was a spindly model which hardly looked capable of performing the great mission assigned to it.

By November of 1847 the press was already in the Mormon Winter Quarters near Omaha—but because of the great demand for wagon space to transport women, children and the priority supplies for settlement, the printing equipment remained behind until the spring of 1849. Only then were six yoke of oxen and three wagons available to haul the press, type, ink and paper.

The three-month westward trek ended on August 7. Meanwhile, Thomas Bullock delayed the coining of gold long enough to make room for the press in his small adobe mint.

The arrival of the printing equipment didn't mean an immediate newspaper for the Saints. Instead, Brigham H. Young, nephew of the Mormon leader, was put to work setting type for official documents, notably a constitution for the provisional State of Deseret. The first actual printing was a bonding form for officers of the government which came off the press on February 7, 1850. Four months later, on June 15, the *Deseret News* became reality.

The paper had eight tiny pages, each 7¼x9¾ inches, but the drama of their appearance magnified them in the eyes of the readers. In the beginning the *News* was an intermittent publication, and one of the major problems was the lack of paper. The editor appealed: "We can't publish without paper; please send us your rags!" Wagon covers, tents, quilts, shirts and petticoats were accepted as tithing and for subscriptions.

The editor also had another plea: "Our printers are in want of eatables; they cannot work without bread . . . bring us your wheat, corn, butter, cheese, eggs, etc." Later the call went out for beaver, otter, mink, martin, wolf and fox furs; also 25 calves and 50 pigs.

From this beginning, however, the *Deseret News* grew and prospered. Meanwhile, other journals were beginning to come onto the scene. These included *Kirk Anderson's Valley Tan,* the first

(Above left) *Kirk Anderson's Valley Tan* was the first Gentile paper to invade Mormon territory. Supposedly, it got its title from the leather produced in the Great Salt Lake Basin. (Above right) The *Manti Herald* was one of several early-day Utah newspapers written laboriously by hand. (Left) This is the original Ramage press on which the first issue of the *Deseret News* was printed. Adam Ramage, a Scotsman in Philadelphia, developed the mechanism in 1796, and many of his presses were used on the frontier.

(Left) Courtesy of the Deseret News

anti-Mormon paper, which appeared on November 6, 1858. As could be expected, the conflicts of philosophy, followed by editorial commentary, often erupted into physical violence. In time, it led the *Utah Patriot* in Park City to comment: "We would suggest that editors who live in a belligerent community make a breast plate of old plate-matter, and wear it under their shirts."

Proof that Utahans took their newspapers seriously was obvious in these bellicose events: A *Salt Lake Tribune* reporter was rawhided; the publisher of the Ogden *Morning Rustler* was tarred-and-feathered and bullies thrashed the editors of the Richfield *Censor* and the *Iron County Record*. This was frontier journalism at its wildest—and the journalists seemingly got the worst of it!

Paper shortages created a crisis for early-day Saints. Rags of all description were collected and hauled to this mill for conversion into various kinds of paper by equipment originally intended for a beet sugar factory.

OUR DIXIE TIMES.

1.　St. George Utah, Wednesday, January 22, 1868.　No. 1.

While the story of the **Deseret News** highlights the history of frontier journalism in Utah, there were hundreds of other papers which came and went, flourished and fizzled. In 1885 Salt Lake City was served by five dailies, and Beaver, with a population of less than 2,000, supported three gazettes at one time, with at least a dozen coming or going in the process.

As in other areas of the Old West, newspapering in the Land of the Honey Bee was not easy. Editors faced most of the obstacles of other frontier regions, plus broad influence of the Mormon Church. The Saints made problems as well as solving them! With supplies costing five and six times more in Deseret than they did in the "States," it was often difficult to make a newspaper pay. An extreme case was the suicide of Horace W. Myers, the 24-year-old editor of the Corinne **Daily Reporter**, who swallowed laudanum simply because he couldn't cope with the financial burdens of publishing.

Less given to defeatism was Scipio Africanus Kenner (at left) whose name turned up in the mastheads of numerous Utah papers, one of which was **Our Dixie Times** of St. George. "Essay Kaigh," as he was known, forsook the practice of law to win prominence as an editor.

149

THE COLUMBIAN.

VOL. I.   OLYMPIA, PUGET'S SOUND, SATURDAY, SEPTEMBER 11, 1852.

THE COLUMBIAN.

PUBLISHED EVERY SATURDAY MORNING, BY
WILEY & McELROY.

Terms.—Invariably in Advance.

For one year, when sent by mail, or taken at the office, $5,00; for six months $3,00.

No paper will be discontinued, unless at the option of the publishers, until all arrearages are paid.

ADVERTISING.

One square (twelve lines or less,) three insertions, $3,00; for every additional insertion, $1,00. A liberal deduction to yearly advertisers.

The number of insertions must be distinctly marked on the margin, otherwise they will be continued till forbidden, and charged accordingly.

AGENTS.

The following gentlemen are authorized to receive subscriptions for "The Columbian:"

Isaac N. Ebey, Whidby's Island;
Henry C. Wilson, Port Townsend;
Balch & Palmer, Steilacoom;
W. W. Miller, Nisqually;
E. D. Warbass, Cowlitz Farms;
S. S. Ford, Sen., Chickeeles;
Chas. C. Terry & Co., New York;
D. F. Brownfield, New Dungeness;
F. S. Holland, Oregon City.

From the National Intelligencer.

The Empire of Japan.

As anything which relates to Japan at the present time may be interesting, I send you the following concise sketch of that kingdom. It is called by the natives Niphon, and was founded about six hundred and sixty-five years before Christ, by Simmu. From him to Sinzakin there appears to have been sixty-one Emperors. After this period, in the year 1142, a change took place. From this time a double chronology commences, including the reigns of the Dearios and the Cubos. The Dearios were military officers, and at one period completely usurped the power of the Emperiors; but a general by the name of Jeretmo being crowned, succeeded in depriving the Dearos of military power. At the present time the kingdom of Japan is governed by an Emperor, with full military powers, a Deario with full civil powers, and a Cubo, or prime minister, who has authority over certain cities, their Parliment, &c.

The kingdom of Japan consists of three large and thirty or forty smaller islands, situated off the coast of China. The largest of these islands is Niphon, the next is Jesso, on the Island of Bungo, southwest of Tonso, is the city or Nangaschi, and near that city is the little artificial island, Disma, on which a Dutch factory is built.

Jeddo, or Yeddo, the capital of the empire, is situated in the midst of a fine plain, in the province of Musea. It is built in form of a crescent, and intersected in almost every street by canals, their banks being planted with rows of beautiful trees. The city is not surrounded, as most Eastern cities are, by a wall, but has a strong castle to defend it. The river Tongag waters it, and supplies the castle ditch; and being divided into five streams, has a bridge over each. The public buildings are on a magnificent scale. The imperial palace is formed by three cinctures, or circular piles of buildings, and encloses many streets, courts, apartments, pavilions, guard-houses, gates, draw-bridges, gardens, canals, &c. In it reside the Emperior and his family, the royal domestics, tributary princes and their retinues, the Ministers of state, many other officers of Government, and a strong garrison. The walls of this magnificent palace are built of freestone, without cement, and the stones prodigiously large. The whole was originally covered with gilt tiles, which are very grand and beautiful appearance of the stately apartments are altered at pleasure, by movable principal apartments are the dence, the Council Chamber Thousand Mats, &c.

The city is under the rule ors, who rule a year.

The next city al city

Emperor. It is near fifteen miles in circumference.

The city of Nangaschi is the Japanese naval depot; but as they have not yet found any use for a navy, their vessels are only in the rough material, and stored away for emergencies.

The kokanse or prison is here. The name means in the Japanese, hell; it has one hundred dungeons and cages. The history of these few cities gives a fair outline of the whole empire. Their private dwellings are small, but neat and ornamental, with small gardens; in this they excel, as they are the very best of horticulturists. A few feet of ground are turned to the very best advantage, as the Japanese understand, by perfectly the art of dwarfing plants, trees, fruits, flowers. They use neither tables, bedsteads, nor chairs; but sit, eat, and sleep, like most eastern nations, on mats.

Almost the first accomplishment learned by them is the art and grace of suicide; the child in the nursery stabs itself with its finger or a stick, and falls back imitative of death; the lover cuts out his intestines before his obdurate mistress, and the latter pours out her heart's blood in the face of her faithless lover; and, in fact, the whole nation, from early youth, revels in the luxury of suicide.

Their trade is, at present, under restrictions, as they only nese and Dutch. T... fostered, cherished, dies of the Japan... tions, particular... Portuguese...

The mechanic... an excel in... are even far su... silks and cott... pan ware an... exports an... iron, ste... than the... copper,... monds...

W...

...St.

...re...
to a...
bert,...
ty fee...
fifteen...
in circu...
called a...
twenty-...
This show...
art of working...
ahead of Christian...
They allow polyg...
gle their female...
males. The nobility ext...
teeth, and supply them with...

The principal rivers are the b... Askagawa—the former so rap... that a bridge cannot be built... latter remarkable for its depth... in fluctuations. The chief lak... is 100 miles long and 21 wide,... ley exists in the interior, fill... obmic gas, and called the Valle... It is covered with the skeleto... ous wild and tame beasts and... Emperor, it is said, often sen... the valley to bring awa... inestimable va... whither...

Misfortunes of Jack Beckler.

Jack belonged to the Irish brig Amelia, a Brazil trader. On the evening of the 25th of August, 1839, the Amelia arrived off Rio, and was immediately noted for quarantine. Jack was one of the midnight watch on that eventful night. The weather was calm and beautiful, and Jack leaned over the forecastle hammock nettings, contemplating the moon which was just setting in the west. Presently he saw a canoe glide out from the shore and he thought he heard...

...The persons in the...
body in the...
ck. Jack...
side was...
ght body...
rods of...
ording...
knew...
ng for...
ecure tho...
s the mys-...
alongside...
ceeded in...
cabin was...
—almost...

...No less than seven hundred valuable diamonds were conceale within that very staff which he had cut in the presence of the Governor himself. Jack's plan was as follows: He would inoculate a particular limb of the palm tree, by cutting a slit in the bark, and slipping a diamond in the issurk. This he would ingeniously fasten until it grew up, and in a short time the place of inoculation would...

...would be a valuabl...
fortune; and had...
to himself antici...
Yankee shi...
devil would ha...
tune to his mu...
ed, and this w...
ing to accompl...
reaching this...
jected again,...
painting in vi...
would enjoy...
again consent...
engaged to J...
would bid ad...
That night...

WRITING FOR THE PRESS.—The following rules on this subject extracted from the London Morning Post, deserves extensive diffusion.

1. Use note paper; because a larger sheet covers the printer's case, and hinders his work.
2. Do not write on the back of the paper, as that doubles the time of printing the article; while one side is being "set up," that is written on the back cannot be "gone on with."
3. Write with dark black ink; for the editor will read with reluctance what he sets with difficulty; and the compositor, for the same reason, will dislike to set it up.
4. Always write in plain bold hands; which are easily set are too ep.

...
...this country to make an effort to open a direct trade with Japan. Commodore Porter, as far back as 1815, addressed a letter to Mr. Monroe on the subject. It was intended to fit out a frigate and two sloops-of-war, and place them under his command. Subsequent events prevented the consummation of this design, but it has been revived from time to time, without being carried out.—But a few years ago, the undersigned drew the attention of Hon. J. Y. Mason to the subject, by the recommendation of a steam line to China, with a view of incidental commercial intercourse, and finally, direct trade with Japan. It would require but small efforts to a commercial intercourse with so shrewd a people as the Japanese, who are alive to commercial feelings. Indeed, Jack declared he would have a shilalah from his favorite tree, "just to keep away the witches, or larrup the lazy mules, as it may be wanted," said he. So he climbed up to the top, and cut off a good stout limb, which he trimmed neatly into a staff, such as he required, and off started the happy jack for Rio in company with a government train.

In order to appreciate fully Jack's ingenuity in all his movements at the Brazilian diamond mines, it should be understood that the convicts are searched and physiced in every possible way to prevent the concealment of the precious gems about or within their bodies. Indeed, Jack declared he took physic enough, during the last week of his stay to last him all the rest of his life.

...himself and wife to return to Rio. The day of their departure at length arrived.—The girl-wife cried and did not want to go so far from home; but Jack talked to her until she consented to go. Just as they were about to start, Jack declared he would...

Washington:

Tale of the Roving Ramage

". . . some women knead dough with gloves on; if subscriptions don't come faster, I will need dough without anything on. . . . Your Editor."

R. B. Darlington
The Molson Leader

AFTER GREAT BRITAIN AND THE United States had settled on the 49th parallel in 1846, the citizens of that portion of the Oregon Territory north of the Columbia River began to clamor for their own government. The intense desire to create the Columbia Territory caused several citizens of Olympia (once known as Smithster) to consider a newspaper to plead their case.

James W. Wiley and Thornton F. McElroy, two argonauts who had failed in the California gold scramble, had greater success in Olympia. Instead of a gold pan, they concentrated their efforts on a doddering old Ramage, and on September 11, 1852, *The Columbian* was born. Oddly enough, before the new paper could get its editorial teeth into its avowed mission, northern Oregon won independent territorial status, with Washington substituted for Columbia.

(Opposite page) This painting by Parker McAllister, *Seattle Times'* artist, depicts the production of Washington State's first newspaper. (Above) The *Cowlitz Advocate* office in Castle Rock during the wooden sidewalk era, circa 1890. (Below) Fiery John Miller Murphy started the *Washington Standard* in Olympia on November 17, 1860, two weeks after his 21st birthday. He operated the paper for more than half a century.

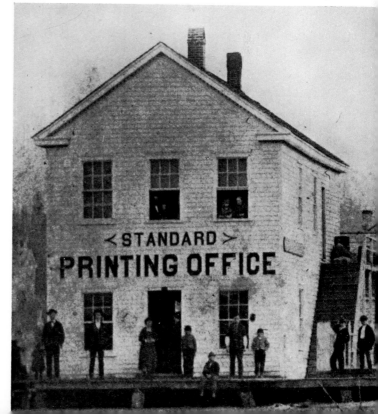

Nonetheless, *The Columbian* introduced journalism to what is now the Evergreen State. However, not until the *Puget Sound Courier* was established in May of 1855 at Steilacoom did the territory have its second paper. Because not many people had wandered northward into the tall-timber country, newspapering had a relatively slow start. Financial support for the first chronicles was meager, and only the revenues from public printing made it possible to operate a paper in the capital city. (The *Courier* in Steilacoom failed within two years.) Meanwhile, *The Columbian* had become the *Pioneer and Democrat,* and as such, dominated the scene until late 1860.

James Wiley, described by the *Puget Sound Courier* as "wild enough to have made his escape from Barnum's Museum of Curiosities," was named the territory's first public printer. In his early thirties, the fiery Irishman was a notorious drinker who, according to historic reports, was always able to dictate clear copy to his compositor even when he couldn't walk. His intemperance got him into trouble with his partners, one of whom was Reuben L. (Bible-Back) Doyle, a printer who was dead set against tippling. Two other partners—Alfred M. Berry and George B. Goudy, who followed Wiley as public printer—each died at 29. Wiley himself survived the ministrations of the Westbrook Saloon until he was almost 40.

On November 17, 1860, John Miller Murphy

(Above) Spokane, like Seattle, suffered a disastrous fire in 1889. The office of the *Spokane Chronicle* was destroyed, but a tent-and-frame structure was erected immediately, a Washington hand-press was acquired, and the paper didn't miss an issue. (Below) Frank M. Dallam (inset) finally got out the first issue of his *Spokane Falls Review* on May 19, 1883, on a borrowed press in Cheney. He had to make two wagon trips from Spokane after a freighter misplaced part of his press.

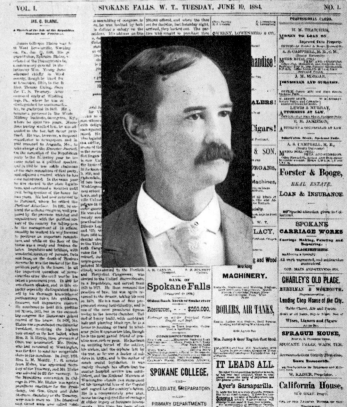

Washington State Historical Society

founded the *Washington Standard,* a strong Republican weekly. Though Murphy himself was never able to win the post of public printer, the change in party domination spelled the death knell for the territory's first newspaper. The *Pioneer and Democrat* (nee *The Columbian*) became a political victim in June of 1861. (Murphy was so sure of getting the public printing that he ordered supplies in advance. Instead, a new paper —the *Overland Press*—got the business.)

While the newspapering of the territory's first decade was concentrated in the southern Puget Sound region, a dramatic boom-or-bust episode was occurring farther north on Bellingham Bay. In the summer of 1858 the village of Whatcom (now Bellingham) suddenly found itself swarming with thousands of gold-seekers enroute to a new rush on the Thompson and Fraser Rivers in New Caledonia (British Columbia). Somehow Whatcom had been selected as the logical jumping-off spot for an overland trail to the diggings. Overnight it became a jumbled mass of tents, mining equipment, 10,000 eager prospectors and one small printing press.

The latter was the property of William Baus-

(Above) Thornton F. McElroy (inset) and James W. Wiley brought newspapering to what is now the State of Washington on September 11, 1852, when they issued *The Columbian* in Olympia. Note that the dateline referred to the region as "Puget's Sound." (Below) The *Intelligencer* was one of Seattle's first newspapers, being established by Samuel L. Maxwell on August 5, 1867. Through absorption and mergers, it ultimately became the *Seattle Post-Intelligencer* in 1881.

Seattle Post-Intelligencer

(Above) This was Seattle in the late 1870s soon after Kirk C. Ward and Benson L. Northrup established the *Daily Post*. Ward was one of the area's most irrepressible publishers, having started several papers. (Left) Ward and his brother, Mark, moved the *Post* into this new building in 1881, just before they lost control of the publication. (Below) This roving old Ramage played major roles in the establishment of journalism in California, Oregon, Washington and Alaska. In Olympia it produced the first numbers of *The Columbian*.

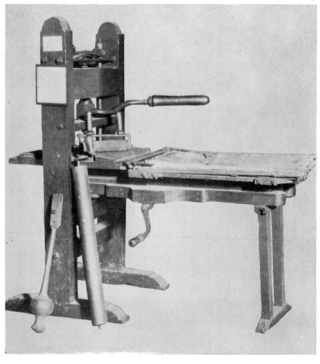

(Below) When the fire of June 6, 1889, destroyed the plant of the *Post-Intelligencer*, the paper moved into the residence of Leigh S. J. Hunt, the *P-I's* manager (above). The next day a tiny bulletin edition announced that new equipment had already been ordered by telegraph. "We have no thought of more than a temporary embarrassment," the paper said. Throughout the Old West fires took a terrible toll of printing plants.

man, former editor of the San Francisco *Sun* who hoped to strike it rich journalistically in or near the new Eldorado. On July 3, 1858, he published the first issue of *The Northern Light* in the community he suggested would be *"the* American town of the North." It took just three months for the bubble to burst. The overland trail was too long, and the strike wasn't as rich as purported. Bausman published his last paper on September 11, and the optimistic *Northern Light* flickered out. In less than ten days, Whatcom was once again a village of less than 200 old-timers who wondered what had hit them as it went by.

In 1852 the tiny village of Duwamps became known as Seattle, but it was eleven years later before it got its first newspaper. On August 15, 1863, James R. Watson printed a few copies of a prospectus paper he called *The Washington Gazette.* This work was done in Olympia, but he took his samples to Seattle where he was favorably received by the local business men. Given

The Seattle Times has a complicated genealogy, dating back to 1881 when Kirk C. Ward established the *Seattle Chronicle*. Five years later the "first" *Times* was created by former employees of the *Chronicle*. The original *Times* survived the fire of 1889, publishing in a tent on Yesler Way after the conflagration. Two years later it became the *Press-Times*. In 1895 the paper was redesignated *The Seattle Times*, and the following year Col. Alden J. Blethen assumed its ownership. (Above) Early home of the "second" *Seattle Times*. (Below left) Colonel Blethen breaking ground for a new *Times'* building. (Below right) Moving day from the *Times'* offices at Second and Union.

assurance of support, he moved his press (the old *Columbian* Ramage) northward and set up shop in the second floor of a building owned by Henry Yesler. The location had two advantages: it was rent-free and the Gem Saloon was directly below. *The Seattle Gazette* first appeared under that title on December 10, 1863.

Watson operated a loyal Union newspaper, and his attacks on Southern sympathizers in the city brought him problems. He was up to the battle, however, and wrote: "Our Union-loving proclivities are offensive to the dunghill chivalry of this region!" When he sold out in 1865, the paper's name was changed to the *Puget Sound Semi-Weekly,* and a new Volume I, Number 1 was issued.

This break is typical of the genealogy of numerous present-day newspapers. The *Seattle Post-Intelligencer* traces itself back to *The Gazette*, with a few bent twigs when the family tree was a sapling. The *Weekly Intelligencer* was started on August 5, 1867, by Sam L. Maxwell, using *The Gazette* equipment which had laid idle after the *Puget Sound Weekly* suspended publication two months earlier.

Another Seattle paper, the *Daily Post,* was established by Kirk C. Ward and Benson L. Northrup on November 15, 1878. It lasted for three years, at which time it was merged into the *Post-Intelligencer* under the editorship of Thomas W. Prosch, already a veteran Puget Sound newsman.

The circulation of *The Seattle Times* was entrusted to this group of eager young carriers gathered in the alley behind the paper's offices at Second and Union. They must have done their job successfully because *The Times* prospered under the leadership of Col. Alden J. Blethen, who acquired control of the paper in 1896.

The city's other surviving daily—*The Seattle Times*—has a similarly complicated genealogy. The same Kirk Ward, who had started the *Daily Post,* founded the *Chronicle* in 1881. Five years later that paper merged with another to become the *Daily and Weekly Press.* The merger, however, displaced many *Chronicle* employees who promptly issued *The Times* on May 3, 1886, the same day the *Press* was begun. Both papers struggled along and survived the disastrous Seattle fire of June 6, 1889. In 1891 they joined forces as *The Press-Times,* the valuable AP franchise of the old *Chronicle* coming along with the former. After several more changes of ownership and financial crises—during which time the paper was run "as a mere incident to a job-printing business"—a final name modification resulted in *The Seattle Times,* first printed under that title on May 11, 1895.

Meanwhile, newspaper activity spread across what was to become the State of Washington in 1889. A repetition of the race to produce the first paper in Denver almost occurred in Walla Walla. Two separate printing outfits arrived at the historic trail town at the same time, with the respective owners each planning to start a paper. Unlike Byers and Merrick of the Colorado drama, however, the two groups got together and decided to combine forces right from the beginning. The first issue of the *Washington Statesman* came off the press on November 29, 1861.

Farther east in the Palouse country, Francis E. Cook (who had started the *Herald* in New Tacoma in 1878) found himself and his wagons mud-bound in Colfax. He was enroute to Spokane Falls to bring journalism to that tiny village. While in Colfax he printed the first issue of *The Spokan Times* (he always left the final "e" off Spokane) on April 24, 1879. It took him six days and 16 horses to haul two wagons the final 60 miles to his destination.

The Times failed, but not so the *Spokane*

Chronicle which was established in 1881 and which battled its opposition over the "missing e." Not long after, another wandering printer-editor —Frank M. Dallam—turned up in Spokane Falls with the intentions of starting a weekly. Unfortunately, the freighter had left behind a critical part of Dallam's press, and in order for him to put out the first issue of the *Spokane Falls Review* he had to make two round trips by wagon to Cheney to have the forms run off. It was a long, tedious process, but the paper finally came out, carrying a dateline of May 19, 1883. This was just in time for the Coeur d'Alene gold rush of that year, a factor which spurred settlement and newspapering throughout the Inland Empire.

Pre-1900 journalism in Washington, while lacking the violence of some other states, was not totally without excitement. In Tacoma in 1886 Sam H. Wall, then editor of the *Evening Telegraph,* was so incensed by what the editor of the rival *News* said about him that he marched to

(Below) When his newsprint didn't arrive in time, Editor Lewis R. Flowers bought a bolt of muslin and printed the first issue of the *Blaine Journal* on "newscloth." The date was April 23, 1885. (Left) In 1890 the promotion-minded *Tacoma Ledger* sponsored a "race around the world" by eccentric George Francis Train (inset).

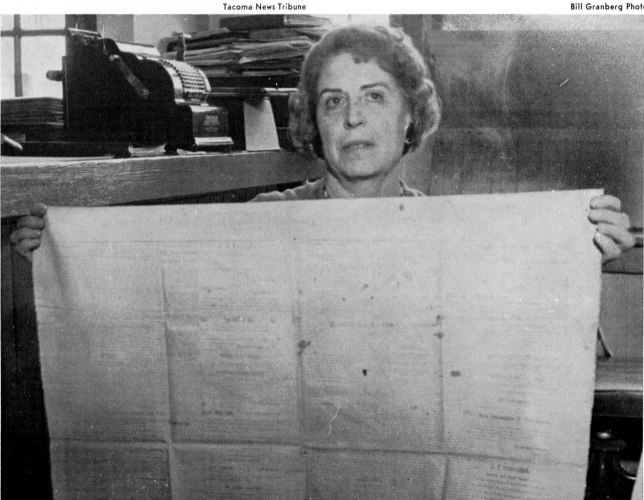

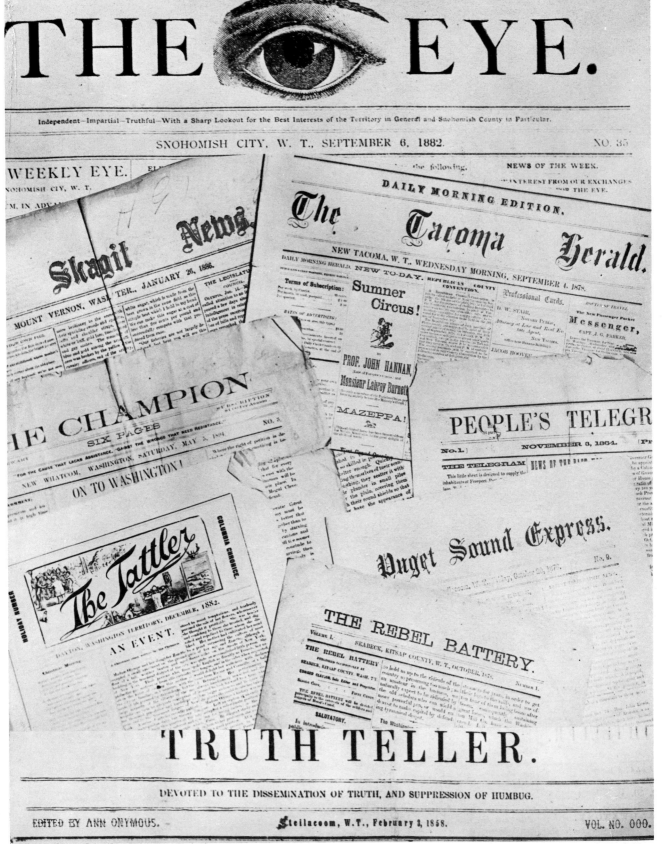

The Seattle Times

A collection of early-day newspapers published in Washington Territory. One of the most unique was the *Truth Teller* (at bottom), edited by "Ann Onymous" and devoted to the vindication of certain military and civil officials charged with being overly sympathetic to hostile Indians. Two issues were printed in Steilacoom in 1858.

Arthur Bernhard

Beriah Brown Family Archives

that paper's offices and took a shot at Herbert Sylvester Harcourt. Fortunately, the bullet was deflected by Harcourt's tie clasp, and Wall avoided a murder charge. Later the same Wall accompanied eccentric George Francis Train on an around-the-world dash in 67 days. The trek —sponsored by *The Tacoma Ledger* in 1890— beat the time of the intrepid Nellie Bly by five full days.

Underscoring the idea that editors were not always paragons of high trust was a case in Fairfield. Local citizens advertised for a publisher, but they were ill-prepared for the young man who showed up. He borrowed money from everybody. In Spokane he married (and deserted) a waitress on a $10 loan. In Fairfield he couldn't pay express charges on the printing gear he had bought on credit. In the end, John Service, the depot agent who was stuck for the freight bill, teamed with a wandering printer to establish the *Fairfield Progress* in 1891. Meanwhile, the garrulous young con-man hopped a freight and disappeared.

In 1892 an editor of the *Morning Olympian* was shot to death by a bawdy house trollop in Seattle. It probably isn't exactly what another frontier editor meant when he wrote: "A newspaper that has no enemies has no friends!"

(Above left) Early-day engravers had to be combination alchemists, photographic experts and mechanical geniuses. One of them was Arthur Bernhard, who founded Artcraft Engraving Co., Seattle, which produced the engravings for this book. (Above right) Few frontier editors cut such a wide swath as did Beriah Brown, friend of Horace Greeley and founder of newspapers in such widely separated locations as Michigan, Wisconsin, California, Oregon and Washington. He was editor of the *Democratic Press* in San Francisco when it was destroyed by a mob in 1865. He later established a paper of the same name in Salem, Oregon. In Washington he edited the *Standard* in Olympia and in 1871 helped create the *Puget Sound Dispatch* in Seattle. The latter paper merged with the *Intelligencer* of which Brown became senior editor. His sons—Beriah and Edward—were also prominent in early Washington journalism. (Below) Home of *The Ledger* in Tacoma, circa 1900.

Tacoma News Tribune

(Above) Small papers which later became suburban weeklies flourished decades ago. Typical was the *Ballard News
Echo* north of Seattle which in 1896 became the *Ballard*

News. (Below) Still farther north, *The Everett Herald*
struggled through its early existence in this unpretentious
frame structure. The date was approximately 1892.

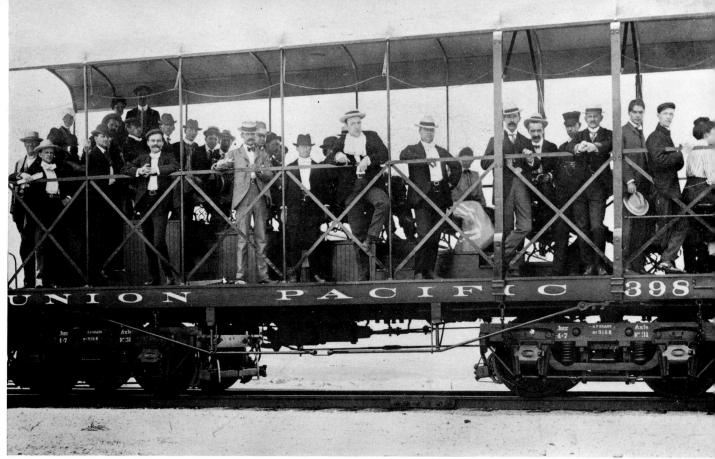

Wyoming:

Sages Amid the Sagebrush

"If The Sentinel is a little thin this morning, just bear in mind that the telegraph office was moving yesterday, the mail from the East didn't come in and there wasn't anybody in town who had enough accommodation to die, get married or have a baby."

The Daily Sentinel
Laramie, Wyo. Terr., 1875

LIKE NEBRASKA, WYOMING WAS A thoroughfare to the Pacific, to the gold fields, to the land of the Honey Bee. Through the valleys of the Platte, the Sweetwater, the Laramie and the Green passed tens of thousands of Mormons, Methodists, miners and other seekers of fortune, freedom and fertile farmlands.

And because of its geographical characteristics, Wyoming ultimately was traversed by the parallel ribbons of steel which carried the Union Pacific Railroad to Promontory Point, Utah, in 1869, to close, for all time, the great gap between the East and the West.

It was the railroad which brought newspapering to southern Wyoming, along with the con-

(Opposite page) Western History Research Center, University of Wyoming

struction camps, strategic sidings and many of the settlements which were to grow into such thriving cities as Cheyenne, Laramie, Rawlins and Rock Springs.

Nomadic fur-trappers of earlier days established little permanency—and the needs for printing presses and such social niceties as newspapers were non-existent. After the beaver fell from favor and buffalo herds were ravaged, the great

Western History Research
Center, University of Wyoming

Hiram Brundage (right) produced Wyoming's first paper at Fort Bridger in 1863 to win a niche in Western journalism history. (Above) The railroads played an important role in establishing newspapers which, in turn, helped them. Reporters shown here are on a press junket over a new line in Wyoming. (Opposite page) The Laramie *Boomerang* had come a long way from Bill Nye's mule to this back shop with an automatic cylinder and electric lights. Editor James Kilgellen is at the stone.

163

Wyoming State Archives and Historical Department

western migration began in earnest. Only then did way-posts and crude forts become the fore-runners of future cities.

One of the first of these was Fort Bridger, established in 1843 on Blacks Fork of the Green River and astride the major routes to the Far West. Twenty years later—after it had already played an important part in American frontier history—Fort Bridger became the birthplace of Wyoming's first newspaper.

Hiram Brundage, of whom little else is known,

printed *The Daily Telegraph,* just two columns on a sheet 6½ by 10½ inches, considerably smaller than the pages of this book. Brundage turned up briefly in the story of the famous "Press on Wheels," but his place in the journalistic history of the West was assured with the discovery of an aging copy of his little paper dated June 26, 1863. Most likely he used an Army press, but whatever his equipment, he produced a news sheet some six years before Wyoming attained separate territorial status.

Western History Research Center, University of Wyoming

Fetterman, Wyoming, in 1886 was an unimpressive shack-town (above) when Bill Barrow, the "Sagebrush Philosopher" (shown at left), established his fledgling *Budget.* (Below) The Saratoga (Wyo.) *Sun* featured a sign over its door advertising baled hay and grain. Sisters Laura and Gertrude Huntington published the earlier *Platte Valley Lyre* which merged with *The Sun.*

Western History Research Center, University of Wyoming

While the Fort Bridger paper is an accepted historical fact, and lead type has been found in the remains of old Fort Laramie, the real center of early Wyoming journalism was Cheyenne. On September 19, 1867, Nathan A. Baker came from Denver to start *The Leader*. Another paper—*The Argus*—also was being published by the time the Union Pacific tracks reached town.

Baker, who at 21 was business manager of the *Rocky Mountain News,* followed his success in Cheyenne by establishing the *South Pass News* in

1868 and the Laramie *Sentinel* the following year. Meanwhile, other papers popped up along the way, and in less than a half dozen years Wyoming had frontier journals in nearly all of its mushrooming little railroad towns.

It was another decade, however, before newspapering in the Equality State made itself felt nationally through the medium of several outstanding personalities. If the poison-pen tirades

(Above) These were the men who published *The Carbon County Journal* at Rawlins, circa 1885. Note the two printers with type-sticks in hand. (Left) Edgar Wilson Nye became one of Wyoming's most famous newspaper personages. The pixie-like quality of his writing gave him a national reputation as a humorist. Nye had arrived in Wyoming with 35 cents in his pocket, intending to practice law. Instead he got a job on the Laramie *Sentinel,* after which he established the famed *Boomerang.* (Right) An interim home of the *Boomerang.*

WYOMING
Monthly Lottery

BY AUTHORITY OF AN ACT OF THE LEGISLATURE.

DRAWS ON THE 30th DAY OF AUGUST, 1875.

Tickets $1 each or 6 for $5.   1 chance in every 3.

Capital Prize, $50,000

SCHEDULE OF PRIZES.

1 Cash Prize	$50,000	1 Cash Prize	1,500
1 Cash Prize	25,000	1 Cash Prize	1,000
1 Cash Prize	20,000	1 Cash Prize	1,000
1 Cash Prize	10,000	1 Cash Prize	1,000
1 Cash Prize	8,000	1 Cash Prize	1,000
1 Cash Prize	5,000	1 Cash Prize	1,000
1 Cash Prize	5,000		
1 Cash Prize	3,000	5 Cash Prizes of $500 each	2,500
1 Cash Prize	3,000	10 Cash Prizes of $250 "	2,500
1 Cash Prize	2,500	20 Cash Prizes of $100 "	2,000
1 Cash Prize	2,500	100 Cash Prizes of $ 50 "	5,000
1 Cash Prize	2,000	200 Cash Prizes of $ 25 "	5,000
1 Cash Prize	2,000	400 Cash Prizes of $ 5 "	2,000
1 Cash Prize	1,500	70,000 Cash Prizes	35,000

70,755 Prizes amounting to **$200,000**

The drawings of Prizes will be made on the 30th day of each and every month during the year.
Persons at a distance can rest assured their interests are as well protected as though they were present.
Persons purchasing tickets or winning Prizes need not be known.
Official Lists of the drawn Numbers will be sent to each person not present at the drawing as soon as printed.
All communications and business transactions strictly confidential.
Remember that every prize is drawn, and payable in full without deduction. These drawings are never postponed, but take place regularly the last week day of each month.
Secure a ticket before it is too late. A chance to win $50,000. This great drawing is conducted legally, honorably and above board by authority of an act of the legislature.
In ordering tickets be sure and write your name, Town, County, and State plainly every time, and without mistake. The errors that occur from this neglect are the cause of much annoyance to the buyer and ourselves. If persons wishing to purchase cannot write their names legibly, let them get some one who can, to do it for them.
☞ To prevent mistakes, a registry of all the tickets sent to correspondents, is kept at this office.
☞ All orders are promptly filled by return mail.
☞ All communications are strictly confidential.
Persons ordering Monthly Tickets, must forward the money with the order, as the time is too short to get returns from Agents.
Money can be sent by mail safely if you fold the Bills carefully in your letter. Seal the letter and write my name, J. M. PATTEE, Laramie City, Wyoming, plain on the envelope. It will surely come safe, or you can send a Draft, or by Express.
Address plainly all orders to

J. M. PATTEE,
LARAMIE CITY, WYOMING.

N. B. The money must accompany all orders for Tickets in the Monthly Drawings.

of personal journalism can be called the "Oregon style," then Wyoming might well deserve recognition for the distinctive, humorous writing of such scriveners as Bill Nye, Bill Barrow, George R. Caldwell and Grant Jones. While they could inflict the lethal barb, generally they weren't mad at anybody, and the papers they served sparkled with their wit.

Edgar Wilson (Bill) Nye—probably the most famous of the lot—arrived in Cheyenne in 1876 with 35 cents in his pocket. Originally intending to practice law, he wound up working for J. H. (Judge) Hayford, editor of the Laramie *Sentinel*. By 1881 he was experienced enough so that a group of Republican business men formed a corporation to back him in a newspaper venture. The paper was named the *Boomerang* after a stray mule which took a liking to Nye. He made considerable

(Above) The Laramie *Republican* was established in 1890 to give that political party representation after the *Boomerang* switched to the other side. The *Republican* ultimately absorbed the *Boomerang*. **(Left)** The J. M. Pattee lottery solved the financial problems of the *Laramie Sun*. E. A. Slack and his crew produced thousands of lottery tickets, and mailing was so heavy it made tiny Laramie a first-class postoffice. Pattee prospered because he never awarded any prizes.

editorial hay out of the fact he put out a newspaper owned by a "stock company" which had its offices in a livery stable. While in Laramie, Nye was also the local postmaster, and his letter to the Postmaster General accepting the appointment was typical of the blithe spirit of his pen. For a job which paid virtually nothing, he wrote to Washington, D.C.: ". . . in my opinion, my being selected for the office is a triumph of eternal right over error and wrong. It is one of the epochs in the nation's onward march toward purity and perfection."

Before Nye had to leave the *Boomerang* and Wyoming because of his health, a young man named Merris C. Barrow went to work in the paper's back shop. Quite possibly he took mental notes while handling Nye's copy. At any rate, when he established *Bill Barlow's Budget* at Fort Fetterman in 1886, he became Wyoming's second humorist-editor. The paper was moved to Douglas three months ahead of the railroad, and there Barlow (as he was best known) also instituted a monthly titled *Sagebrush Philosophy* which brought him national recognition.

A third light-hearted editor—"Colonel" George R. Caldwell—was known as the "Lurid Liar of Lander." Supposedly a pun on that nickname resulted in the title he adopted for his new paper in Saratoga: the *Platte Valley Lyre*. He was a paragrapher of note and a spinner of tall tales.

(Above) Edward A. Slack was one of Wyoming's busiest journalists, publishing or editing papers in South Pass, Laramie and Cheyenne. He was the son of Esther Hobart Morris, militant suffragette who made history when she was named first woman justice of the peace in the nation in 1870. (Left) Remnants of Wyoming's past.

In the latter field he was challenged by Grant Jones, editor of *The Dillon Doublejack* around the turn of the century. Jones, a promising young metropolitan reporter, had lost a battle with John Barleycorn and came West to try again. In the shadow of the Sierra Madre Mountains he wrote his animal fantasies which are now classics. His One-eyed Sceaming Emu was a bird which could swallow itself in one frantic gulp. The Coogly Woo was a six-legged creation with a sharp tail which, when pursued, simply stood up on its tail, whirled rapidly around and bored itself into the ground.

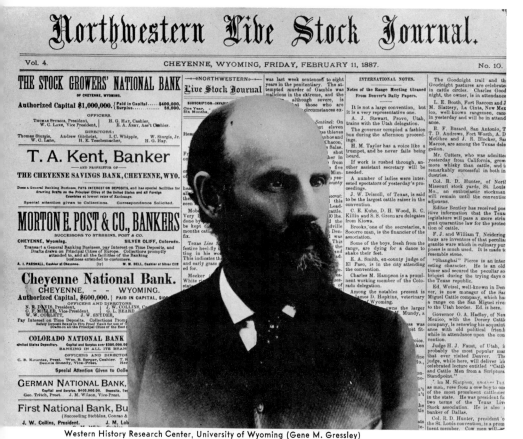

Northwestern Live Stock Journal.

Vol. 4.   CHEYENNE, WYOMING, FRIDAY, FEBRUARY 11, 1887.   No. 10.

Western History Research Center, University of Wyoming (Gene M. Gressley)

Asa Shinn Mercer rightfully belongs in the histories of at least four western states. In Washington he is most noted for the Mercer Girls, the ship-load of marriageable young ladies he brought from Boston for the wife-less men of the Pacific Northwest. He was also first president of the University of Washington. In 1876 he went to Texas where he published the **Bowie Cross Timber**, the **Vernon Guard**, the **Wichita Herald** and the **Mobeetie Panhandle**. Earlier he had established **The Oregon Granger**.

It was in Wyoming, however, that Mercer wrote "The Banditti of the Plains," the classic of range warfare which brought him lasting fame—but at the time, he paid dearly. His paper—the **Northwest Live Stock Journal**—was closed. The cattle barons he indicted for wanton murder seized and burned his books; the plates were destroyed, and Mercer himself was jailed. His revelations, however, constituted a remarkable example of fearless journalism on the frontier!

CATTLE MEN READ THIS!
Great Inducements to those who wish to
Ship Cattle on the U. P. Railroad!!

Having entered into special arrangements with the U. P. R. R. Company, by which I can ship Cattle East at greatly reduced rates, and having selected a point between Carter and Church Buttes Stations some ten miles East of the former place, near the junction of the Big and Little Muddies, and having Constructed Commodious Lots and Extensive Enclosures, and the Company having put in a Switch capable of holding 40 Cars, I will be Prepared to Commence Shipping on or before the 15th of the Present Month, and will be able to promptly ship any Number of cattle that may be Offered.

Persons driving Cattle from Montana and Idaho, and passing by Soda Springs and the Bear Lake Settlements, will cross over from Bear River to the head of Little Muddy and follow down that stream, over a good road, to within a mile and a half of the junction of the Little with the Big Muddy, where they will cross a bridge and find a rich pasture, extending many miles; good water & perfect security for their stock, within convenient distance of the stock yards.

The cattle yards are in an enclosure of some 400 acres, and stock scales and all conveniences for shipping will be furnished. If parties do not wish to ship themselves, I will purchase, at good prices, all shipping cattle that may be offered. As cattle are now bearing excellent prices East, it would be well for persons to bring their Cattle forward as soon as possible.

For further particulars, address

W. A. CARTER,
Fort Bridger, Wyo. Ter.

Fort Bridger, July 2, 1877.

Of course, Wyoming journalism wasn't all frothy and light. Serious problems abounded, and the frontier newspapers tackled them one way or another. There were county seat fights, vigilante committees and the great struggle for women suffrage. Boomerism became a factor along the main rail lines and the spurs. The "Johnson County Range War" erupted editorially in Asa Shinn Mercer's *Northwest Live Stock Journal* in Cheyenne and spread to other papers. A racial problem was spelled out in the first issue of the *Lusk Herald:* "No Chinese need apply!" The same paper also commented: "Lusk needs a carload of marriageable young ladies."

For all the seriousness, though, the "Wyoming style" emphasized the quixotic and the titillating. Perhaps Bill Barlow had the right idea when he wrote: "Live, laugh and love—there'll come a time when you can't!"

Fading into oblivion were boom-and-bust settlements like Bear River City, Old Tub Town, Bothwell and Bonanza. Like many other Western ghost towns, they live on only in the tattered pages of the newspapers they spawned—and which died when they died.

The Press on Wheels.

FEW STORIES IN THE SAGA OF Old West journalism can match that of *The Frontier Index*—the peripatetic "Press on Wheels."

Like many tales of pioneer endeavor, it has been colored in the re-telling and punctuated by conflicting "facts" and a few historical inaccuracies. But basically the story is this:

Following the Civil War, two brothers from Culpeper County, Virginia—Legh R. and Frederick K. Freeman—came to Ft. Kearney, Nebraska Territory, following their release from a Union prison camp. At Ft. Kearney a tiny paper called *The Herald* had been issued sporadically since 1862 when it was established by Moses H. Sydenham. The paper and the Army field press were acquired by Seth Mobley, a soldier in the Seventh Iowa Cavalry, and Hiram Brundage, the post's telegraph operator.

Legh Freeman, who succeeded Brundage at the telegraphy switch, also ended up with the printing equipment and *The Herald*. At Kearney City ("Adobe Town") the Freemans changed the paper's name to *The Frontier Index* and thus set the stage for the drama to follow.

When the Union Pacific began to push its rail line westward, the little newspaper became a journalistic vagabond. With the construction camps, it followed the trail across Nebraska, into Colorado, Wyoming and Utah. Bombastic, somewhat eccentric Legh Freeman became its chief functionary. He issued a volatile sheet from tents,

(Top right) Courtesy of Kemper Freeman
(Bottom right) Western History Research Center, University of Wyoming

(Top) The reversed column rules—a universal mark of mourning in early-day journalism—commemorated the death of Legh Freeman's wife the day before the Butte City, Montana, edition was printed. **(Bottom)** Legh R. Freeman as a young man when he and his brother were operating the West's most nomadic newspaper.

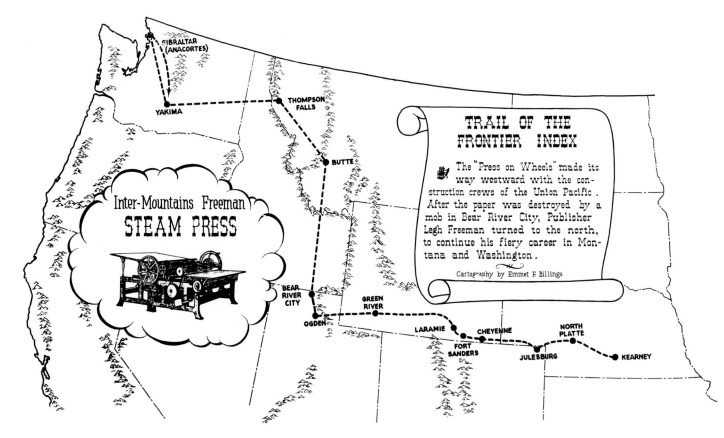

TRAIL OF THE FRONTIER INDEX

The "Press on Wheels" made its way westward with the construction crews of the Union Pacific. After the paper was destroyed by a mob in Bear River City, Publisher Legh Freeman turned to the north, to continue his fiery career in Montana and Washington.

Cartography by Emmet F. Billings

(Above) This map shows the trail of "The Press on Wheels" and the known publication points of other newspapers established by fiery Legh Freeman. The steam press in the inset was a feature boasted by the meandering publisher when he was involved in a newspaper war in Butte, Montana. (Opposite page) Legh Freeman in later years when he ran unsuccessfully for mayor of North Yakima, Washington.

rail cars, log huts and other assorted shelters. At least once (at Julesburg) he printed *The Index* on brown wrapping paper; always the production problems were difficult because of the temporary conditions. One advantage Freeman did have was the availability of telegraph news all along the route. It made his papers more up-to-date than most. He got advertising when he could and supplemented his income with job printing.

Freeman later boasted that he published his paper at 14 terminal towns along the Union Pacific right-of-way. Few of these sites have been verified, since copies of *The Frontier Index* from 1866 through 1868 are extremely scarce.

Ironically, *The Frontier Index* did not make it to the end of the line. At Bear River City, Utah, Freeman's bellicose editorials were his undoing.

His violent anti-Mormon stand and his exposure of Credit Mobilier frauds resulted in the destruction of his plant in November of 1868. While *The Index* nameplate was revived, at least briefly, Freeman's subsequent publications in Utah, Montana and Washington operated under varying titles.

Wherever he went, red-headed Legh Freeman created a stir. In Butte he got into lengthy legal problems when he issued *The Daily Inter-Mountains,* a paper with the identical name of an existing Butte publication except for the hyphen and the final "s." His career came to a close in Washington State where he was involved in publishing, politics and promotion. He was always flamboyant, aggressive and rigidly positive in his beliefs. Though he died almost in obscurity in Yakima in 1915, his contributions to newspapering on the frontier cannot be underestimated.

THE FRONTIER INDEX

VOL. I.   JULESBURG, FRIDAY, JULY 26, 1867.   No

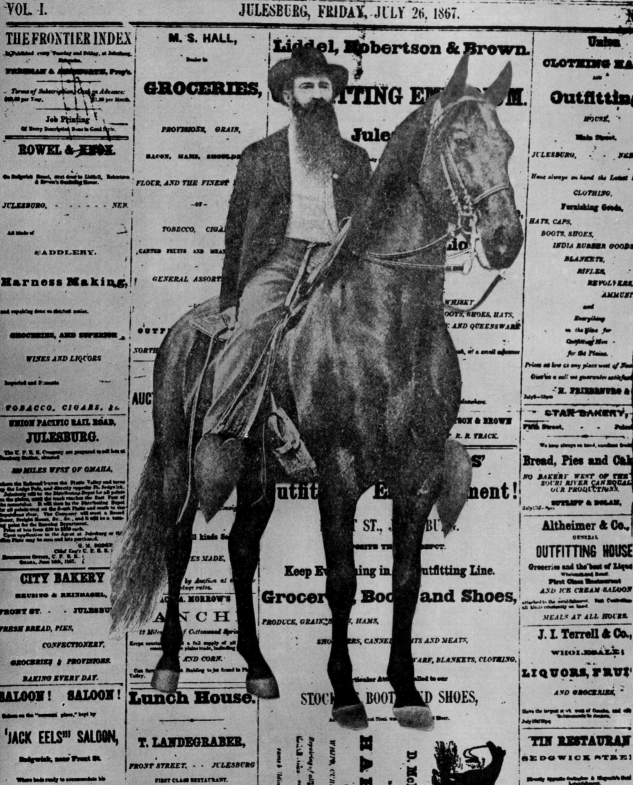

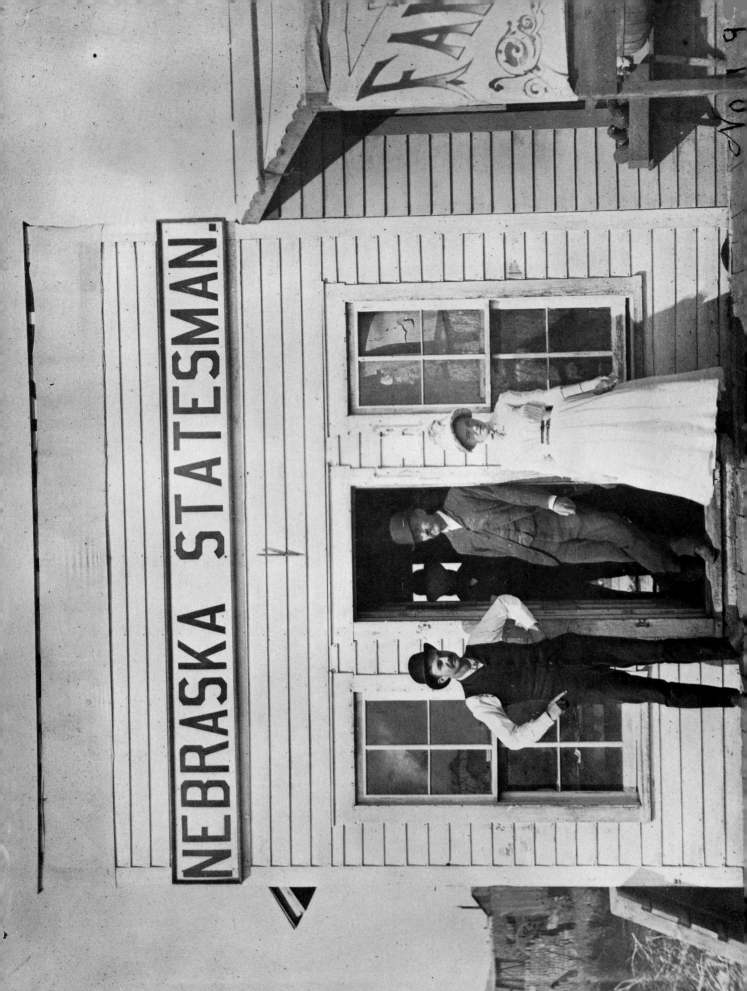

Throughout the West, in newspaper offices and job shops, women compositors were present. Few of them hoisted heavy forms or operated man-killer presses, but they were valuable assets in the somewhat delicate but monotonous job of typesetting. (Opposite page) It is difficult to know whether this young lady in Broken Bow, Nebraska, is prouder of her Sunday bonnet or her type-stick. (Above) A Seattle job shop, circa 1900.

Printers in Petticoats.

"Bustles made from the Gazet (sic) are not affected by electric wires."

J. W. "Watermelon" Redington
Heppner, Oregon, 1888

Frontier newspapermen quickly determined that "the hand that rocked the cradle" could also justify a line, ink a form and—if necessary—pull an impression on a Washington or a Ramage.

Many an ink-smudged young wife worked beside her tired husband in the continual battle against their weekly deadline. And, in time, more than a few determined widows assumed control of the newspapers and printshops which, in some instances, had been directly responsible for their widowhood.

Initially, women were not involved in frontier journalism any more than they were in the front ranks of the Argonauts, the pioneer lumberjacks or the railroad construction crews. But as soon as permanent settlements were established, families were united and new ones formed, with the obvious result that ladies were available to help out in the shop as well as in the home.

For one thing, there was a great deal of dexterity involved in picking the tiny lead characters of agate, nonpareil, minion and brevier out of a California job case. Women not only could hold their own in this department, but often they delivered more ems per hour than male type-sling-

(Opposite page) Nebraska State Historical Society

Smasher's Mail.

VOL. I. NO. 6.   **TOPEKA, KANSAS, SATURDAY, MAY 18, 1901.**   **PRICE 5 CENTS**

"PEACE ON EARTH, GOOD WILL TO MEN."

MRS. CARRIE NATION

A Home Defender Who Defends.— Leader of the Greater Smashing Reform Crusade.

CARRIE NATION'S VIEW OF KAN- SAS.

I felt when this blasphemer was asked to speak at the Sunday School State Convention by the president. Poor "goose" of a man, if I may thus apol- ogize for him! I sent in a request to speak ten minutes but was not allowed. Why? This is a puzzle. But one thing I do know. The man who would have Stanley speak, would not wish me to. We do not belong to ——— And this Stanley is in ——— poison at the Chatau ——— our State. I am remi ——— ments of Casca in spe ——— man populace at the t ——— be emperor. "If Star ——— their mothers they w ——— no less." Cæsar was ——— live to do that, but S ——— and stabs men, women ———

A Royal Boo ———

We heartily approv ——— The czar in banishi ——— the noblest man of the ——— has cast a stigma upor ——— that will be effaced on ——— tion. "The head and ——— fending" was that of ——— in Christ to the comm ——— too late in the centu ——— heads to act as dictators of other men's consciences. The following reply of the Count to the Czar will be fresh in the memory of his grateful country- men when czardom and popedom shall in turn be banished from earth. "Why will you fight with what you can not subdue by force instead of cov- ering your name with imperishable fame by treading the way of justice? You protect injustice, sire.

"Free the peasant from the brutal tyranny of the officials; give him equal rights with other ranks; do away with the present police system, which de-

he deceived the people into electing as their governor Stanley, the wolf in

mation to prove my insanity. When he told me he did not take my hatche out of my hand at Moeser's he did lie When he refuses to give up my proper ty to which he has no right, he is thief.

———

Foreignism.

Fred Worthington, Shelbyville, Ind.

Carrie Nation of Medicine Lodge, nemesis of Kansas saloon-keepers, greeted the readers of her anti-booze newspaper with a borrowed slogan: "Peace on Earth, Good Will to Men." And she meant to attain that peace if she had to whack up half of Kansas with her trusty hatchet. The clarion call of prohibition and wom- en's suffrage was instrumental in attract- ing many female do-gooders into the field of journalism where they could use the power of the press in their causes.

this outrage. I shall demand it as my right in all my cases hereafter. Who will deny me? Mark the man that does

THAT WHISKY JURY.

When I secure the names of the men who sat on the jury that convicted me on May 14th, in Topeka, for the "ma licious destruction of property," when I was the law abiding citizen, while they were the anarchists, I will name in Smasher's Mail next issue that these men may be marked as fit for treason strategem, and spoils. Such men are

The Kansas State Historical Society

ers. Moreover, a good, dependable female com- positor was far cheaper than an itinerant "tramp" —and she was less likely to hide a bottle behind the furniture cabinet. What the ladies had to say

about "type-case hands" can only be imagined. Crude inks made of lampblack and oil had lots of staying power, especially around the fingernails.

In the 1880s women started to emerge from

David C. Duniway

this lowly beginning. The San Francisco *Chronicle* boasted a lady reporter—Mrs. Florence Apponyi Loughead—in 1879, and elsewhere the fairer sex was becoming more and more evident in other than the smudge and drudge departments.

Nothing brought women more to the forefront in newspapering, however, than "causes." Suffrage and temperance lured the ladies out from behind their organdy aprons to do battle—and one of their most effective weapons, they soon learned, could be a newspaper.

There was, for instance, Abigail Scott Duniway, "mother of equal suffrage in Oregon." Strong-willed and talented, Mrs. Duniway in May of 1871 established the *New Northwest,* devoted to political, financial and social equality for women. Sister of Harvey W. Scott, able editor of the *Oregonian,* she was a facile writer, capable of wielding the so-called "Oregon style." Besides operating her newspaper, Mrs. Duniway trod the lecture trail, cared for a husband in poor health, raised a family of six and wrote books. She sold the *New Northwest* in 1887, but in the nineties she was again an editor, this time of the *Pacific Empire,* a weekly established by Miss Frances Gotshall.

(Above) Abigail Scott Duniway, "mother of equal suffrage in Oregon," is shown in this old photo with a copy of the *New Northwest* which she published from 1871 to 1887. (Below left) There was little glamour for a woman

printer in Clinton, Oklahoma Territory, circa 1900. (Below right) In 1900 the *Elma* (Wash.) *Chronicle* made its weekly appearance because of the nimble fingers of Nettie Watson at the type case.

Oklahoma Historical Society

Washington Newspaper Publishers Association

Nebraska State Historical Society

(Above) This young lady was a typesetter for the Anselmo, Nebraska, *Sun*. Though she held a type-stick, she was probably dressed for the photographer rather than work. (Right) Faye Fuller had two distinctions: she was the first woman member of the Washington Press Association and the first of her sex to climb Mt. Rainier. She was on the staff of the Tacoma *Daily Ledger* when she made her ascent in 1890. She also assisted her father with a weekly publication called *Every Sunday*.

Meanwhile, Catharine Amanda Scott Coburn—Mrs. Duniway's younger sister—was also making her mark in Oregon journalism. After working on the *New Northwest,* she became an editor of the Portland *Evening Telegram* from 1883 to 1888. After that she spent a quarter of a century as associate editor of the *Oregonian*.

The Scott sisters were somewhat unusual, but they weren't the only women to grace editorial chairs in the Old West. Three years after Mrs. Duniway started the *New Northwest,* Mrs. Laura DeForce Gordon bought an old press and issued the *Daily Leader* in Stockton, California, supposedly the only daily newspaper in the world edited by a woman at that time.

In Colorado Caroline Romney had a press hauled over snow-covered trails from Leadville to Durango where she issued the first number of *The Durango Record* on December 29, 1880—in a

tent with a saw-dust floor. As editor she was shot at by desperadoes, and during a particularly hostile period her printers worked fully armed with rifles and revolvers. In one of her papers, she answered a fellow publisher on a more domestic issue: "The rumor . . . that the editor of this paper is about to be married is without foundation. In fact, we can't afford to support a husband yet."

Before the Civil War, Indian girls in what is now Oklahoma published *The Cherokee Rosebud* at the Park Hill Female Seminary at Tahlequah. Later in the nineteenth century, Lily and Dolly Wright were editors of the *Beaver Herald* in the Panhandle Country. Another pair of sisters—Gertrude and Laura Huntington — edited the *Platte Valley Lyre* in Saratoga, Wyoming. In Utah the *Women's Exponent* had female typesetters and editors who had learned the trade while working in the shop of the *Deseret News*. As a matter of fact, the first "news boy" of the Mormon paper was not a boy at all, but the adopted daughter of the editor, Dr. Willard Richards.

By 1886 it was estimated that some 500 women worked on the editorial side of American news-

Washington State Historical Society

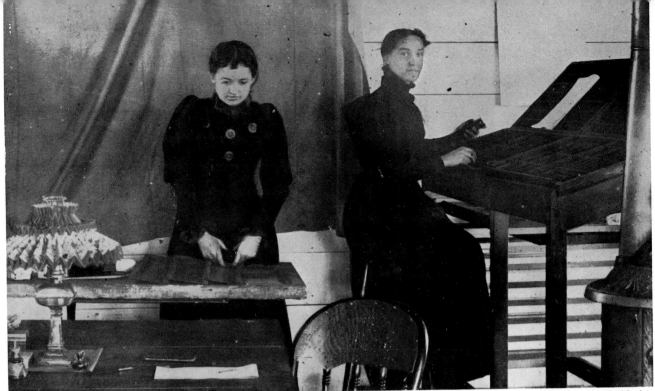

(Above) In Quenemo the *Kansas Workman*, established in 1882, was hand-set by "working women." The canvas on the wall helped keep out prairie breezes. Not all shops had kerosene lamps with fancy pleated shades. (Below

right) In Wyoming the *Platte Valley Lyre* of Saratoga was published by the Huntington Sisters—Gertrude M. (shown here) and Laura C. There were several such sister combinations in Old West journalism.

papers. A year earlier the Women's International Press Association had been formed. But nothing gave greater impetus to the distaff side in journalism than the exploits of Elizabeth Cochran, the famed "Nellie Bly" of the *New York World*. Her wild dash around the globe in 1889 paved the way for a surge of femininity into newspaper offices across the land.

But in the small frontier weeklies, there was little need for Nellie Blys. Women simply took their places beside their husbands at the type cases and the roll-top desks. They saw little of the glamour or excitement experienced by the lady reporters on the metropolitan dailies. There was simply too much space to fill, type to set and impressions to pull.

Like their male compatriots, the "printers in petticoats" put in long hours for little pay and

WANTED
IMMEDIATELY

A young Lady between the ages of 10 and 15 years to learn the art of Type Setting. Must be Quick and Active, able to read common writing and not Afraid to Work. Steady employment guaranteed when competence is gained.

For particulars apply to

J. W. CARPENTER.

This notice in the St. George, Utah, *Evening Telegram* indicated the need for lady compositors in 1879. Women were in demand at the cases because they were generally sober, dependable and dexterous.

177

(Above) Early-day photographs of newspaper staff members usually included several women. In the 1880s the *Visalia* (Calif.) *Weekly Delta* was published by this handsome septet. (Below) Militant ladies with axes to grind operated numerous papers in behalf of suffrage and temperance. *The Idaho Woman*, which appeared in Caldwell in 1897, was typical.

less recognition. Not only that, they faced scorn and scandal as jealous men tried to stop their invasion of the newspaper plants. Even William Allen White wrote: ". . . in our office which was free of the female taint we gossiped bitterly and salaciously about the foreman and the printer girls of the other shop. Perhaps all this was the intuitive fear of a tide of feminism."

No matter what the die-hards said or thought, women gradually found a place for themselves in the print shops of the Old West—and in spite of the dire predictions, the Fourth Estate did not collapse in a flurry of gingham curtains, perfumed soap in the washrooms and bouquets on the feed-boards!

In the beginning, society news—if there was any—was written by men. They worried little

(Above left) The telephone and the typewriter revolutionized newspapering techniques as much as the Linotype changed printing methods. This young lady—probably a secretary rather than a reporter—worked for *The Denver Post*. (Above right) Indian Territory (now Oklahoma) had newspapers in the 1840s. In later decades both boys and girls were trained to set type and operate presses in tribal schools. (Below) This is how *The National Police Gazette* pictured a fighting female editor of a frontier newspaper in 1882.

about the niceties of etiquette or the social caste of their subjects. They covered dances, "bees," lodge meetings, weddings and birthings with much the same language as they reported the arrival of a shipment of flour or the affairs at the county courthouse.

Sometimes they got carried away a little. In 1881, for instance, the Portland *Oregonian* included the following verse amongst its society notes:

> Mary had a vaccine scab
>   Upon her snow-white arm;
> She warned her beau to this effect
>   For fear he'd do it harm.
> But when they came to part that night,
>   She gave a mighty grab
> And whispered, "Hug me awful tight
>   And never mind the scab."

Obviously, no *lady* society editor wrote that!

Gradually, however, the distaff side found more and more editorial duties as newspapers departmentalized. "Sob-sisters" and home economics editors became standard equipment. After that, newspapering was not quite the same!

(Opposite page) Youthful news boys of early-day Willis-ton, North Dakota. (Above) One of the exhibitors at a trade fair in October of 1890 was *The Seattle Telegraph.* Well-scrubbed carriers handed out free copies—but in spite of the promotion activities, the paper did not survive for long. (Below) For a few pennies a week, youngsters religiously hawked the local newspapers on street corners and at public gatherings.

News Boys' Hey-Day.

King Patrons, good morning! a happy New Year
To you all! may peace and prosperity cheer
Your lives and your labors through all coming time;
May you always be "flush," not lack the dime—
Or the quarter, or more—to gladden and cheer
The Carrier's heart at the dawn of each year.

Carrier's Address
Rocky Mountain News, 1860

COUNTLESS HUNDREDS OF RAG-A-muffins and knicker-clad youngsters contributed immeasurably to the success of journalism in the Old West.

Their assignment was simple: deliver the fresh-ly printed journals to readers anxiously awaiting the week's news. Like postmen, they traveled through mud and blizzard and downpour, when sidewalks were rare and houses were wide-spaced. For a mere pittance they braved unruly dogs and sometimes unruly subscribers.

(Opposite page) State Historical Society of North Dakota

Old-time printshops had a magnetic attraction for young boys and girls alike. Often there were more potential "devils" and newscarriers under-

(Above) Labor organizations played a vital role in the history of western newspapers. Even young news boys paid dues and went to union meetings. (Below) Carriers for *The Spokesman-Review* in Spokane, Washington, delivered their papers afoot and on horseback. Bicycles replaced the latter as streets were paved and urban areas grew.

foot than the editor would have preferred. Yet, the youngsters filled a definite need. With survival being more of a factor than profit, publishers barely could afford the few coppers they paid their small helpers. The "glamour" of the newspaper office (no matter if it were a tent or a sod hut) made up the difference.

News boys weren't always "boys," however. In some areas—notably gold camps—where papers sold for $2 or more apiece, the transactions were seldom assigned to urchins. Many of the early delivery routes were too rugged for tiny feet. In Nevada, for instance, 45-year-old Thomas Starr won a small measure of local fame for the diligence and physical stamina with which he served *The Territorial Enterprise.* For two and a half years—seven days a week—he trudged up and down Alder Gulch and Gold Canyon on his daily mission. He started when *The Enterprise* came off the press at 3:00 a.m. Eighteen hours and 35 miles later he returned to his bed to rest up for the next trek. This was obviously not child's play!

Ill paid as they were, news boys of the frontier

(Above) *The Denver Post's* Boys' Band was a popular promotion gimmick. Other newspapers had similar activities for their carriers. (Right) Because even small towns had more than one paper, news boys faced stiff competition. This 1897 calendar implied that *The Republican* was easier to sell than its rivals.

era always looked forward to New Year's Day. That's when the editor provided them with their annual Carrier's Address (see page 101), usually an elaborately printed verse which the youngsters gave to their subscribers. Not only did these addresses wish the reader a prosperous year ahead, but they hinted—often quite broadly—that it would be a good time to remember the news boy with a token, preferably cash!

In the print shops, carriers and "devils" (often the same ink-stained boys) were constant victims of the traditional practical jokes of the trade. They were sent after slug-stretchers, left-handed quoin keys, checkered ink and italic shooting sticks. They all learned the menace of type lice. Yet, in the small communities, especially, it was a mark of distinction for a small boy to be accepted at the newspaper office. No trial, taunting or tribulation could take away from that!

(Above) News boys of *The Los Angeles Times* were all bedecked for a parade when this photo was taken prior to 1900. (Right) *The Crusher* in Cripple Creek, Colorado, depended upon this young man to get circulation among the miners of the lusty gold camp. *The Crusher* once startled its readers by coming out in gold ink, long before such inks were generally perfected.

Gradually the frontier newspapers evolved into "modern" journals. The one-man printer-editor began to fade away. In the larger cities—like Portland, Oregon—the papers developed versatile staffs, with trained writers rather than the unschooled type-slingers who produced many of the West's first chronicles. This picture shows the newsroom of the *Oregonian* in 1894. Note the bad lighting and the absence of typewriters.

Index

In the beginning, the journals of the Old West printed "news" which was weeks old. The short-lived Pony Express gave promise of reducing the lag to mere days. Then came the telegraph which made transcontinental communication possible. Telegraph desks—like this one of the *San Francisco Examiner*—became vital to most dailies.

San Francisco Examiner Photo

By the turn of the century, the Linotype had revolutionized newspaper production in plants large enough to afford them. The *Medford* (Ore.) *Mail Tribune* installed two of them. Meanwhile, the rest of the shop retained the appearance of a decade or two earlier, cluttered, ill-lighted, poorly heated and drab.

Old West Newspapers

Union Pacific

Job printing ranged from simple business forms to elaborate posters such as this one which announced the completion of the transcontinental railroad.

Literally hundreds of newspapers came and went in the early days of San Francisco journalism. This building housed the *Daily Evening Post* in 1884.

THE SITKA POST.

Vol 1.　　　SITKA, ALASKA, FRIDAY, OCTOBER 20, 1876.　　　**No. 1.**

CRIMEAN SKETCHES.

No. I.—A SORTIE.

No one in the advanced trench of the left attack on the night of the 11th of May, 1855, ventured to contradict the oft-repeated assertion, "Well, this is rain!" for it was rain—rain that percolated freely through mackintoshes, meandered through your hair, poured down your back, and laughed to scorn the devices of London bootmakers;—rain that reduced the contents of your haversack to a conglomerated mass of wet crumbs, pork fat, and morning papers;—rain that poured into your flask, and positively refused to let you drink brandy neat;—rain that put out the match of the candle of the "Officers' Patent Camp Cooking Lamp," destroying all visions of hot tea, and caused the owner, who had placed faith in the drawing representing an officer shaving himself by the brilliant light of the lamp, to wish that the said officer would cut himself severely;—rain that pattered up the mud into the soldier's mouth who foolishly bleared his eyes in the hope of lighting a few frizzling fascine chips;—rain that rendered the chambers of the mortars a desirable dwelling-place for young ducks, and that caused the magazine man to be universally envied;—rain that caused small avalanches of mud to fall upon the recumbent head of any unwary man who took refuge under the traverses;—rain that made the back of Captain Smith's government-issued sheepskin great-coat, worn with the woolly side

method for procuring instantaneous light vanished with a flicker like the gasp of an expiring glow-worm;—rain that made the men declare, walking about with the following articles of saturated clothing—viz., one mackintosh cap, one forage cap, one woollen nightcap, one chamois leather waistcoat, one jersey, one mackintosh overall, one boat-cloak, one belt, one great-coat, one comforter, two pairs of drawers, one pair of mitts, one pair of woollen gloves, one pair of leggings, one pair of trousers, two pairs of socks, one pair of stockings, one pair of knee boots, in addition to their arms and accoutrements—was worse than hard labor;—rain that made the sailors ask, "Why don't you artillery look sharp and set the town on fire," and brought forth a rejoinder from the gunner, "Shut up, you marine artilleryman!"—rain that poured a steady flow of salt into the sunken powder-boxes ironically supposed to contain water, in reality containing a fluid in which artillerymen generally had dipped dirty canteens (with a substratum of grease) and muddy water-bottles, and the fluid had a leathery twang when it shunted in from the water-bags of the Land Transport Corps.

When the storm is at its height, just as the relieved sentries have sunk down on the mud with a squashy groan of utter weariness, a cry is heard; three musket-shots that follow are succeeded by startling yells. All spring to their feet;—cries of "Stand to your arms! Stand to your arms!" resound from mouth to mouth; the out-sentries rush in through the embrasures; men fall over the trails of the guns; Lieutenant Jones calls out, "Here

Though Alaska isn't included in the 17 states of the Old West, journalism got an early start there, too. The first paper seems to have been a manuscript sheet called *The Esquimaux*, produced in 1866 by John J. Harrington while the area was still Russian America. *The Sitka Post* (shown here) was reputedly the first printed paper in the territory. It appeared eight years after American occupation.